Promise and Heartache

❖

Promises and Heartache

Copyright © 2011 Juan Carlos Perez

Cover Design by Juan Carlos Perez,
http://www.cpdigitaldarkroom.com

Published in The United States of America

ISBN: 978-0615489872

Promise and Heartache

Juan Carlos Perez

Acknowledgements:

I'd like to thank every person that's ever been there for me and I'd also like to thank every person who's ever been a total fucking dick. Without both of you I wouldn't have all these pent-up emotions to write about.

I truly appreciate all the good friends I have that support me through everything, unconditionally staying beside me through my imperfections. I want you guys to know I appreciate everything.

This one's for you.

Poetry

❖

3LhC+2J--->Lh3J2+3C

A single replacement reaction,
That's what we could call it.
A simple chemical reaction
Between 3 elements and no spectator

We could even go as far
As to say that the chemical equation was right.
Yet I'd like to stick to the facts,
And point out that it was indeed wrong.

A stupid mistake on my part,
I should have seen it sooner.
You see, according to the activity series,
Nothing can kick me out. I'm most active.
There is no element known that,
Could ever break us apart

3LhC+2J--->Lh3J2+3C
Gladly I can say this is wrong
3LhC+2J--->NO REACTION

J. Carlos Perez

A Love Lost

What happens with a love lost?
A broken heart?
A shattered dream?

Does it evaporate like alcohol
On a warm summer day?
Or does it linger in
The air like the stale taste
Of a decaying corpse?

Is a love lost
Forever gone
Or can you store it
Inside a fragile crystal encase
To be later removed
And relived once again?

Only to be broken again.

A New Dream

Oh my love how I miss you
It's like we are further than years,
This love that I feel cannot be extinguished with oceans,
My illusion of you is simply so strong,
That by simply closing my eyes,
I see a new dream were only your eyes and lips exist

About Me

I straighten my hair everyday,
Have been since December.
You're the one who first suggested it,
It's something you should remember.

I listen to Secondhand Serenade
While I shower and shave.
Looking back at things
I first heard them on your page.

I like to sing along
With songs and make song covers.
Some say I have a rad voice,
You say I sing like Mister Rogers.

I didn't believe in equality,
I used to think some people were barbarians.
You showed me different,
You showed me how we are all just humans.

I watch many chick flicks
And even some on Lifetime.
People would kill to have
A mind like mine.

I have and IQ of 142
Yet how did that help me in the end.
My smart intellect didn't help
Me in again seeing my best friend.

❖

J. Carlos Perez

Afraid

I see the light at the end of the tunnel
But I keep walking backwards,
Afraid to see what's at the end.

The birds flap their wings towards freedom
But I shackle myself down to the ground
Afraid to let go of what I've known.

The breeze pushes time forward slowly
While I keep living in the past
Afraid to see good things die.

Cancer patients look forward to every day
While I piss away time by not fully living.
I'm stuck on repeat saying, "Will you miss me too?"

Life keeps on moving towards better things
As I stand here
Afraid to say goodbye

All Alone

The phone rings
No answer
Two rings
Echo with no answer
The third ring
The phone is picked up
No answer
I'm all alone

The power goes out
I turn on my computer
The power goes out
I turn on the television
The power goes out
I turn on the radio

I hear a voice

"Forever", it says---
I'm all alone
"Forever", it lies...
I'm cold and heartless

Half-truths of nothingness
Spill into the airwaves
Leaving me...
All alone

J. Carlos Perez

All Goodbyes

I remember every coup d'oeil
You gave my way
With your central heterochromatic eyes
And realize it was all goodbyes
From the beginning.

❖

Am, Was, Were

As the day grows old
I return to what I've grown
To call my home.
To the hallowed shell
And the darkened walls.

If you asked me who I am,
I couldn't tell you
For I don't know myself.

As the day grows old
Once again I'm shown
That no matter where I roam
In this world--a constant hell--
In the end we all fall.

If you asked me who I was,
I'd tell you it doesn't matter,
You and I have reached the end.

❖

An Obsessed Fool

To say now, my love,
That I have forgotten
You, would be a lie
Most foul. The mere mention of
Your name makes my day
And stops my breathing momentarily.

If only I could have you momentarily
For myself again, my love,
I would show you how I have not forgotten
You. Though our lives were full of lie after mingy lie
I cannot think of
Anything other than you that makes my day.

I still remember the day
I lost you. I had you in my sights momentarily
Then you disappeared behind a veil of lies. My love,
Not one of your details goes forgotten.
I cannot lie
And say I don't remember the days of
Bliss, or that I don't think of
You each and every day.
Thinking of you makes my day better even if only momentarily.
Then the truthiness of our shallow hopeless love
Makes me drink myself into a land of the forgotten
But even then, I'm living a lie.

My love, I am tired of living a lie.
My life now consists of
Two packs of cigarettes a day
Followed by a superfluous amount of liquor. Momentarily
I'll forget about our love
But our past simply cannot be forgotten.
Tell me, my love, have you forgotten?

❖

13

J. Carlos Perez

Angles Dancing On Satan's Pond

So deceitful
Were the both of us
I lied to you
And you lied to me
Both hoping the other
Would never catch on

We both shared a deathly affinity
For lust and lies
Who would've known
That we were one,
We were one in the same
Shameless...
And so deceiving

What an irony
Yes what an irony it was
When I told you the truth
When I told you I loved you
You thought
I was lying

As Flowers Do

We meet again, a casual glance
Through a crowded market, a flame
Lingers from our past romance

You approach me, hands at your side
Restraining themselves from an embrace
You've tried to convince yourself our love has died.

As flowers, your fragrance intoxifies
The air, mesmerizing my five senses
All it would have taken was a look in your eyes.

Our shoulders brush, a feeling like dawn
Creeping its grasp over the dormant land
Shakes my body, but just like that you're already gone

❖

J. Carlos Perez

As Good A Day As Tomorrow

I say hello to you,
For the ten-hundredth time
From inside this cell of self-denial.

I tell myself,
I will get over it.
I tell myself,
I will be fine.
But slowly I'm beginning to lose my mind.

Witch each passing stanza,
With each written poem.
I pour out my feelings for you,
But you,
You don't seem to notice.

I cannot go on like this.
I need to get away,
From these strings of hypocrisy.
I've been lying to myself,
And I for one cannot take it anymore.

I've been pushing this away for far too long.
I've been leaving it for a tomorrow that never comes.

Today, well
Today is just as good as tomorrow will be.

I love you less than yesterday,
And more than I will tomorrow.

At 18

He gave up on love at 18 years old.
His hearts been broken so many times before
He decided it wasn't worth his time.

Three years and a half, I am told
The time he hasn't had a girlfriend to adore.
Oh how loves a crime.

His heart tells him yes
But he says no.

He gave up on love; he gave up on his heart

He gave up on love at 18 years old
The last person he loved was a total whore,
Threw him away like a dime.

He is now 25 years old
Still thinking he is better off than before
I know this because his life is mine.

He heart says yes
But he says no

He is afraid they'll kill his heart.

❖

J. Carlos Perez

Back Home

When I came back from war,
I told myself I wouldn't be back again.
Just what the hell is all this for?

My friends are crying,
My mothers dying
And all if this back home
While I'm off fighting
While I'm off killing
For a man who's lost control.

When I came back from war,
I lost my faith to the knife.
I questioned what the hell is all this for?

Why do I feel like I've been lied to?
Why do I feel like I'm more needed at home?

Beginning To Learn

13 Years
468 Weeks.
2340 Days.
16380 Hours.
982800 Minutes.
58968000 Seconds.
All that time spent
Learning on how to excel in life
And yet it feels like I learned nothing.
Maybe the real learning begins later.
Once you step out into the world.
23 hrs. have passed since
I took my final steps
In that horrid school
And I've already
Learned so much.
I learned how
Much I'm going
To miss you,
My friend

❖

J. Carlos Perez

Boat In A Bottle

I feel enclosed
Surrounded from all around
The air gets thicker and thicker
And I am unable to make a sound

Everyone stops to stare and look
But offer no sign of help
It's like a story inside a book
Were loneliness is all I have ever felt

I'll bang on the walls
Trying to break free
But I grow weak and my strength falls
I am held tight by the hold of thee

I feel like a boat in a bottle

Bootrom Exploit

Tell me you're kidding
I'll take anything but this.
The poison of your kiss
Has my heart beating
Out of place.
The look on your face
Reveals you're not lying.
This whole moment of bliss
Should not exist.
Yet, why is it I keep falling?

Bracelets

I've been wearing these strings
Around my wrists
Holding on to what I've known
Afraid to lose all memory
Of the one thing in life
That's had an influence in
Changing me into the man I am.

Breaking Away

I got my nails painted black,
Twenty dollars in my wallet.
I'm walking out, no looking back.
I want to make it to Hollywood.
Were the girls come fast,
And party's thrown like they should.
I want to get away from here,
The same old things in this small town.
I want to go fall head over heels.
My name will be known,
And my face will be recognized.
On every commercial it will be shown.
I just want to break the monotony.
Be something no one expects.
I want to be anything, except a celebrity.

J. Carlos Perez

Can You See The Pain?

As I look into
Your eyes.
The ones that
Captivated me from the
Beginning.

I see
Emptiness,
Hollowness.
Your eyes
They seem dead
To me now.

You look into
My eyes.
Can you see the pain?
It's there
You should see it.

You're the one who caused it

Caring

Hair the color of pencil shavings
Eyes as bright as a million suns
Such a great friend
Since just a few months ago
Until she seemed to stop
--Caring—

❖

Christmas In September

In a car,
Outside of your house,
Realization hit me in the face.
There is no snow in September.

❖

J. Carlos Perez

Cold Hearted Whore

You think you deserve
Better than anyone else.
And guess what?
You do.

I agree you deserve
A little something extra
To showcase your
Grandiosity.

You deserve a token
For all the effort
You put in to make
Me feel so stupid and miserable.

To tell you alone simply
Wouldn't be enough
Because you'd shrug it off
And slime on over to the next "Guy of the Week"

You deserve a little better.
That's why I named a
Poem after you.

Again.

❖

Compassion

Every year thousands of kids are born around the world
Many having very little to live by
While others have thousand dollar pillows

I feel compassion for these kids
Who will never be given a chance to be something
They'll never have the same opportunities as you

I was once told
Never to cry or feel sorrow for strangers
But in this day in age
It hurts to see a homeless person
Especially when the holidays come around

J. Carlos Perez

Compromise of our Chauvinistic Hearts

Lets come to a compromise
So that we can both be happy.
You promise to be nice,
And promise to let me be.

Promise never to look for me
Ever again in your life.
Promise you'll never go crazy at the
Sight of seeing me with a wife.

Promise that you'll never raise
Your hand in anger with a knife
If I forget about you through the days
Through the struggles and through strife.

Me, I promise not to get mad
If you break your promises, actually I'll be glad.

❖

Confined

I awaken it's dark
Absolute darkness
I move, I can't
The walls are confined
I push, No budge
Where am I trapped?

I close my eyes, try to remember
It's all such a blur
I search in my mind, nothing
I know not where I am
I scream and I cry
This is not happening, Why?

Above on fresh ground
You shovel and shovel
With each passing second
The hole becomes smaller
You're burying my love
You're burying me....

J. Carlos Perez

Constellations

I look up and I see
A clear mirror of your eyes
Lost in thought, lost in the sea
Of stars in the skies
I visualize the importance you've had on me.

Printed perfect memories
Play in the sky, dreamy
Mixes of incongruent formalities
Lit by the plum blue and berry
Reds of the stars like these

If I could fly and touch the moon
There's so much I would do
I'd write your name with the brightest stars
To show you how truly special you are.

Count the Letters (20, 23, 44, 50, 57, 79)

Lost among these jumbling letters
Humbly hidden among the vast lines
A hidden name lay to be found

Also among all the letters
Kindly scattered from place to place
Lay another message, sleeping well sound

Effortless thought will get you nowhere
Lest you're a cryptic agent
Need another clue? Look at the title

Craters On The Moon

There's no use living life
Thinking of the negativity,
When in fact,
Life is full if ups and downs.
You have to accept and find a way
To live through the strife,
Thinking of them better days.
It'll all be better soon.

Your life is yours,
Do with it what you can,
Minute after minute,
You're in control of every single aspect.
Don't let them haters
Bring you down with their roars.
Keep on escalating, triumphing, making craters
While high up on the moon.

❖

J. Carlos Perez

Dear Stranger

This photograph
Is the last thing that I have.
The only memory left
Of how things used to be.

I don't even know
Who you are anymore.
All the thing's you stood for
Have shattered and left me cold.

You used to be kind.
You used to care.
Now you put down people
Like you are better than them.

You have become a stranger
In my eyes.
Someone I don't know.
Someone I don't want to know.

I will keep this picture
Locked up tight in a safe.
Protecting the real you
From what you've become.

Hey Stranger!!!
Look at yourself in the mirror.
What do you see?

Dear Void In My Heart

I built a home in the hole I dug
And learnt to live on bare necessities.
I invited you in to share some company
But it's time to say goodbye with a hug.

Wish me luck, I know I will need it.
I'm taking a chance and filling you in
But fear not, I will probably need you again.
Dear void in my heart, just forget it.

What's the use of kicking you out,
When everything's already been figured out?

I was born to live with you in my heart.

Dreaming

If it's a dream that you want
You wont find it here, go on now
Carry on living like we've never met
Go on now, living a lie.
Someday you'll open your eyes
And realize, that life's not all about
These dreams you've been dreaming about.

J. Carlos Perez

December Missed Its Goodbye

I've tried to find a solution to this
But there is no easy end to this.
December is long gone and summer is here.
Yes, it is what you fear.
Love is at the door with suitcase in hand.
Just like December, it's long past its end.

Diamonds Lost At Sea

Diamonds hanging in a summer sky,
A mocking reflection of your eye,
Sit idly between the idea of you and me.

Oh, how I wish on this late day in July
That troubles would disappear for you and I
But it seems as though all hope is lost at sea.

The hands of the sea have come and taken my
Muse, my will from me with no goodbye.
The sea has taken away the idea of you and me.

Oh, how I wish I could swiftly fly,
Acquire a diamond to the likes of your eye
But alas, it seems as though they too are lost at sea.

Did I Change?

I wasn't always like this
A lonely cold-hearted fool
I used to be better

I don't know when I changed
Perhaps it was after the pain
Or perhaps...I never changed at all

Dust

Treated like a throwaway,
An unwanted flower left to wither
Away and rot,
She buries her face in the dust;
Dry tasteless dust.
Her dry useless life;
Like dust;
Blows away in the wind.
Her life blows away
With the insults and putdowns.
She can't shed tears.
She is incapable of feeling;
Numb to the bone,
Dry to life.
Like dust she'll blow away
Into oblivion.
Dry tasteless dust.

J. Carlos Perez

Don't Want To Be Like You

I,
Always looked up to you
And I,
Always thought you were amazing
But I,
Don't want to be like you

I,
Don't want to walk around
With my ego stuck on high
And I,
Don't want to be the epitome of misery

I,
Always praised you as being great
And I,
Always cared what you thought
But I,
Don't want to be like you

I,
Don't want to look in the mirror
And see a prelude to death
And I,
Don't want to be a whore

I don't want to be like you

❖

Edit Undo

They say that the human mind
 Is the most powerful computer in the world.
They say that it can solve
The most advanced problems that were ever dreamed of.
They say many great things about the human mind
And very few people have any problems with it.
I have only one, only one that I can think of,
How the hell do I get to edit undo.

11:11

You are a truly amazing person
And without you I don't know what I'll do.
Probably wish every day and night at 11:11
And hope that my wish comes true.

I'll wish upon every shooting star as well
Hoping that maybe that star
Could take my message to God
And bring me closer to you.

Everyday I'll wish
And hopefully one day again
You I will see again.

J. Carlos Perez

Entrapped

Your eyes glimmer with every glance
Like that of the star filled skies above
So full of life and high on romance
Nature's creation of things to love

You speak so soft and fair
And the melodic line
It's like a musical tennis match where
The players dwell in love divine

Nobody, not even the wind has such gentle hands
Like those that you use to hold me
Better than my own hands
I like them more than I like me

The lines of this poem so full of....
Of love, your kiss, those hands, those eyes divine
Let my amorous lines court thou my love
And leave your hands entrapped in mine

Every Time

Every time I see brown size four converse
They remind me of how much I love you.
Every time I see a broken heart
It reminds me of how much I hate you.
Every time I hear Landon Pigg's "Coffee Shop"
It reminds me of how much I love you.
Every time I see a happy couple
It reminds me of how much I hate you.
Every time I watch "A Walk To Remember"
It reminds me of how much I love you.
Every time that I see you
It reminds me how much I...

J. Carlos Perez

Everything Is Going To Be Alright, Right?

The world stops in place,
Colors intertwine like an over exposure photograph,
Sounds become smells,
And time defies all laws of physics.

My eyes dart from side to side,
Like jack rabbits in heat,
Trying to take in all that's happening,
In a fraction of a second.

I force myself to think of happy thoughts
Something to take me away
From this imminent catastrophic event.
My family. My best friend.

Although a clear cliché,
My life flashes before my eyes,
Highlighting the best parts.
All this before I can even blink.

Another law of physics breaks
As I float upside down,
Spinning a full 180
Before landing on the ground.

I close my eyes for the first time
And think ever so clearly
"Is this really happening to me?
Is this where it all ends?"

Sparks begin to fly
Like the fourth day in July
Bright bright red covers the empty space
Like fireworks in the sky.

My arms, blocking my face,
Are pelted by broken glass
And banged against a roof which isn't supposed to be so close,
It's not supposed to be so close to my face.

I realize I'm holding my breath and think
"Is this my last breath?
Are these my last words?
Everything's gonna be fine. Right"

The car comes to a stop
A strong smell of gas infiltrates my nostrils
But I'm tired
Just let this end.

I close my eyes for a second
As silence takes over the night.
I am tired and broken.
Just tell me everything's gonna be alright.

❖

J. Carlos Perez

Falling

Don't you let go of the things
That make us whole, keep me from
Falling apart and I promise I'll
Keep you from falling in love.

Falling Asleep

Don't worry about falling asleep;
Things can only get better from here.
Fall into his arms.
Let your mind fall into the deep
Darkness. He can still hear
Your prayers and will keep you from harm.
Don't worry about falling asleep.
Lift your heads and cry away your pain.

When you read this
Wherever you may be,
Just know you're not alone.

Don't be afraid to fall asleep.
Things can only get better from here.
Fall into his arms.

Fantasy Life

The whole world is a stage
Where people exist because they dream.
I dream so much that I
Do not know whether this world is real
or if I am living a fantasy life inside my head.

Four You

Walking down the sidewalk,
Passing by the streetlights,
Pride held high and head hung low,
I'm in a place I thought I'd never be.
It's taken me so long to stop and see
There's no use for the shouts
And fights. You're worth so much more to me.
If you were to ask me about
The memories and our past
There'd be a lot of ghosts to let out.
There'd be conversations about how fast
Things culminated and we both went about
On our own paths and solemn walks.
Passing by these street lights,
I realize just how far I'd go
To have you here with me.
Everything I do,
Has been for you.

J. Carlos Perez

Final Hour

I've seen my world come down
Right by the seams
You took my crown
And called it your own.

It's time for me,
To regain my throne
And gain back my life.

It's time for me,
To make it on my own
And gain back my life.

I've been running in circles
Making you believe I cared about you
(But this is the final hour
There's no going back from here)

You tried to make yourself
My god, a divine spirituality
You must be kidding yourself
I won't ever let you call me your son

It's time for me,
To cast you out
And gain back my life.

It's time for me,
To stop the screams and shouts
And gain back my life.

This is the final hour, Say your goodbyes

Getting Girls To Notice Me and A Million Other Things I Suck At

Getting my homework done.
Driving with two hands instead of one
Hell I'm better off with none

Playing Rock Band while dealing with sleep depravation
Paying in cash at gas stations
Avoiding cell-phone vibrations
Even conducting operations

Throwing pots in under one minute

Paying attention in class
Cutting the jungle like grass
And making relationships last

Found Love

Love entered my life the day that I meet you
Before that it was all an illusion that I never knew
I searched for love in all the places I could muster
So many wrong places and when I got tired of looking It was you
that found me
You opened my eyes to a world I thought no longer existed Only you
knew how to bring out the best in me
You awaked the love that was dead in me

Now everything is clearer and distinct I love you so much that I
would do anything to please you and make you the happiest woman
Thanks for coming in my life
Forever I'll love you

J. Carlos Perez

Gone Are The Days

Gone are the days
In which I believed
Your every word.

Gone are the days
In which your eyes
Captivated my world.

Gone are the days
In which your kisses
Left me perplexed in place.

Gone are the days
In which I could stand
Looking at your face.

Gone are those days

Todays I don't feel hate.
I feel a strong
Sense of relief.

Goodbye Present Love, Hello Future Pain

A day with a million suns
Would be bright, no less
But it would fail in comparison
To the eyes you posses.
Tell me why oh why
You cant be here with me
We have been apart for oh so long
And you I long to see.

We were once the best of friends..
We were once the best of lovers-
3 long years we dated off and on
Never hiding behind any covers.
This time your leaving me for good,
Going away to another town.
I will say goodbye with a smile,
But never my love will I frown.

Goodbye my love

J. Carlos Perez

Graduation Goodbyes

Remember all the times we argued and fought,
The times we made fun of each other.
 I can still remember,
The first day we met.
We didn't know each other,
 But we treated each other like brothers.
We had lots of misunderstandings,
But tried to fix what was broken
 We had lots of wonderful memories together,
And now our time is up,
 We have to say goodbye.
Goodbye for now, I'll miss you,
We've been through so much,
Sometimes I still have no clue,
 If we'll really keep in touch.
But please do not cry cause we WILL be in touch One day,
eventually, if not tomorrow
Will you miss me past tomorrow,
Will you know me at a glance?
 I'll try hard to remember,
Every moment spent with you,
Memories might not last forever;
But the friendship we share we share will make it through.

❖

Graveside Love

Her smile woke the dead
The day she smiled at me
I never thought I'd feel it,
All those butterflies in my stomach

I took her cold hand in mine
Sharing my warmth with her
I wanted to take her home with me
Yet I could not do so
For she smiled at me from inside her coffin

❖

Have You Here With Me

I dream about you every night
It's a constant battle with the sands of time
If I close my eyes I see you there,
Standing rigidly mocking me.
I just want to be next to you
No matter if it kills me
I just want to be there with you
Even if it means living with my eyes closed.

I'll keep on dreaming
Of our better days
The days in which
You stood by my side
I just want to be next to you
No matter if it kills me
I just want to be there with you
Even if it means living with my eyes closed.

❖

J. Carlos Perez

Hello Heartbreak

Shy?
Who me?
Paste tense honey,
My love isn't ashamed
To be expressed anymore.

Touch me,
Go ahead,
Don't be afraid of
Getting hurt.
I'm only a danger
To myself.

I know
What I'm getting into
And I don't care.
I'm tired of turning
Myself down.

How will I face heartbreak
If I don't put myself
Into the situation?

Hello heartbreak,
Here I come.

Here For You

No matter how bad
A terrible day
You're having girl
I want you to know
I'm here for you
In every possible way

I've been over the mountains
I've made it through the rain
I've fallen down
And made it back up one knee at a time
I know what it's like to be down for the count
Left for defeat down on the ground
And girl, I know things will be okay

Girl I know life may seem hard at times
But I want you to know you can call me no matter the time
And I'll stay with you until
you've turned your frown upside-down

I know sometimes I may seem so far away
But I want you to know I'm only seconds away
Just close your baby blue eyes
Drown you're mind of the negativity and remember my words

No matter how bad
A terrible day
You're having girl
I want you to know
I'm here for you
In every possible way

J. Carlos Perez

Hey There (Pretty Girl From Dobson)

Hey there, pretty girl
Won't you come with me?
We'll tour the world
By land, air and sea.

And if things don't work out
We'll come back to town
And we'll forget about
All the wonderful things we found.

You're just a pretty girl from town
Who has me head over heels.

I know the other guys
Might be braver than me at times
But honestly, tell me this.
How many would write you a poem that rhymes?

Hey there, pretty girl
Won't you give me a chance?
I'll embrace you with a twirl
And we'll get lost in the trance.

You're just a small town girl and
Already many poems have been written for you.
How many of those guys
Would write a poem for you?

You're just a pretty girl from town
Who has me head over heels

How Easy Is It To Forget

How easy is it to forget?
When you said you truly loved me
and said that you would always be there
How easy is it for you to forget?
The compassion, the warmth
My every caress
Is it possible to have forgotten
all that in a matter of days?
Is it possible that after
all that has happened between
Us,
We simply turn our backs and disappear?
How easy would it be to just forget?
Forget I ever meet you, and forget
about all the magical moments,
I spent at your side
That would be foolish...
Yes it might be easy to forget
but is it what we truly want?
Do we really want to forget about the other?
Or do we simply want the pain to subside?

❖

J. Carlos Perez

How Can You Tell?

How can you tell
If the woman you love knows you exist?
Maybe she thinks of you
Maybe she doesn't
How can you tell?
Perhaps she feels the same way
Thinking about you
And how she wished you love her
Yet again, how can you tell?
Possibly you love one another
But are too timid to tell each other
How can you tell?

❖

I Believed

It's 2 in the morning and I still can't sleep
Your voice playing in my head still cuts me deep
"Never had a chance" you say
Do you honestly think that's the best way
To say goodbye?
Without knowing why
Just yesterday you said we'd see it through
I swallowed your words. I believed in you

❖

I Blame Gravity I Fell For You

Don't ask me why I love you,
Don't ask me why I care.
I couldn't answer you even if I wanted,
There really is no reason there.
It's almost as if I trained myself
To fall for people over the simplest whim.
Indeed I can hear my heart chanting
As the lights grow dim.

"Ready your weapons, We're going to war.
Lower your guard, We're letting them win"

My eyes looked over you
With a graceful glance
And I instantly thought
"Holy shit, I've got a chance"
I know I did
This to myself,
But I still blame gravity
I fell for you.

❖

J. Carlos Perez

I Know

Though tonight I still have my life, I know
I know tomorrow my rifle I will stow
And I know tomorrow we will all inhale despair
Death bells can be heard in the air

I know that's bloods smell in the mist
And I know desolation won't be missed
My tired limbs pray for ceasefire
But are left yearning in desire

But I know

I know one day soon,
I will rest in Flanders Fields

I May, But

I may,
One day grow old and gray
Wither away with each passing day

But,
I will never forget you
Never will I lie as you do

I may,
One day lose touch with reality
Go insane after losing you, oh what a calamity

But,
I will never fade away
I'll be with you in soul till my dying day

Today I die...

J. Carlos Perez

I Never Said I Had An Elephants Memory, I Said I Would Never Forget You

Staring off into the mirror that sits in front of me.
I see a person that I simply don't recognize.
Is it possible that I have changed so much?
Was your influence so great that it still persists?
Comeback to me! Just let things be
Like they were when I stared off into your eyes
Dreaming of our future and the such.
I don't know if my love will every seize to exist.
As I look into my own eyes
I wonder if I will ever be able
To close them and not see you...
And not see you.
In a few years you will call me a stranger
Not knowing I was the man you once loved.
That will be when I will make my move....
I will rekindle the flame that once was.
Where fire once burned,
There will always
Be embers ready
To be lit once more.

I Tell Myself

To the left of me is the sketch I drew
You know, the one that looks like you.
That looks like you...

To the right of me is my lonely pen.
The one that fell the day you left.
The day you left...

I tell myself that I'm over you.
I tell myself that I can now move on.
I tell myself....
I tell myself you meant nothing to me.
I tell myself that I don't care.
I tell myself....

In front of me is a blank paper.
Ready to be turned into another sketch of you
A sketch of you...

To the back of me is a solemn path.
The one I walked when you left.
The day you left...

I tell myself that I'm over you.
I tell myself that I can now move on.
I tell myself....
I tell myself you meant nothing to me.
I tell myself that I don't care.
I tell myself....

I try to tell myself all these things,
But I just...
can't...
Get over you...

57

J. Carlos Perez

In The End

And in the end all that's left is the unavoidable feeling of longing.
The realization of loves inability to motivate,
To stir an ire within you to fight for us.

And in the end all that's left is the unattainable feeling of perfection.
The endless winter nights, your name whispered by the wind
And your eyes reflected by the moonlight on the cold still waters.

And in the end all that's left
Is a realization of deserving so much more.

Infamously Lonely

Infamously lonely
I sit in my room
Thinking about
All the things we've been through

I pull down a star for you
Each and every night
Been doing it since you left my side.
Now there is no more left to enjoy.

My closet is full
Of bright shinning stars.
Saving them up for the day you return
I'll put them back up and say they came with you

Infamously lonely
I sit in my room
Thinking about
All the things we've been through.

Believing in dreams
Is what its about.
I have many dreams/ all about you
Directly meaning/ I believe in you

I believe

J. Carlos Perez

Insecurities and Questions; You and Fig Newton's

Has an end ever been found for the question "why"?
Why so?
Why is that?
Why?

Do writing poems and stories about you, make you hungry for more?
Do you even realize when a piece is about you?

Are you thinking of me at this very second?
By asking if you're thinking of me, does it automatically make it a
yes?
If you answered no to the previous question are you wrong?

Could I possibly drown in the fountain of eternal life?

If a car is going at the speed of light and the driver turns on the
lights,
Would the lights hit him in the face?

If an unstoppable bullet hits an impenetrable shield,
Which one would come out victorious?

Am I so sure of myself I can't help but feel insecure?

Am I a Fig Newton in some bodies' imagination?
If so, what does that make of my love for you?
Is it "real" love in a non-real world?

Does any of this even make sense?
If I told you there was a hidden message in these lines,
Would you go back and try to find it?

Did you find anything?

❖

It's About Two

Sometimes I worry dear
What am I to write about
When all has been said
And read about you?
Though I thread little on the fear
I know someday far out,
When all words have left their lofty bed,
There will be nothing left to say.

I know the idea sounds bleak
And my concession disappointing
I know one thing I shouldn't do
Is hold on with a hardened grasp.
 At the untimely peak
Of my stylistic writing,
When I've run out of things to say about you,
I'll leave you loves task.

For I can say blissful lines,
Loves about two, not just mine.

J. Carlos Perez

Just Call it A Day

I wake up everyday,
It seems on the wrong
Side of the bed.

Since you been gone
It seems all I do
Is scream and get mad.

I'm tasteless
And restless.
I'm a big sack of shit.

I want to say
That I still love you
But I cant.

My feelings for you
|HATE|
As you can get.

If I ever
Told you I loved you.
Forget I said it
And call it a day

Krakens and Wizards

So, it seems as though
We have forever been departed.
It seems as though
we will never share in each other's comfort again.
I don't worry...

Though the occasion does bring sadness.
I know that one day
When Krakens and Wizards
Again roam the Earth.
We will come together once again.

Impossible you say,
I think not!
My wand may be beyond repair,
But my pet Kraken is still alive.

One of these days
I will embark on a journey.
In which the good guy will get the girl
And everybody will live happily ever after.

I will roam the Earth
And rescue you from the
Dark prison that you live within.
I will break the curse put upon your heart.

It will be just us two
And my pet Kraken.
A Kraken and a Wizard
Accompanied by a Goddess herself.

J. Carlos Perez

After A Day Like This

After a day like this
I feel like there is nothing,
that could take me back to my perfect bliss.

Everything that I once cared for
is gone. Vanished in thin air.
How could you just walk out and close the door?

After a day like this,
I just want to go home,
and find another person to whom my heart lease.

❖

Last Time

If this was the last time I could see you
I would burn your image in my eyes, so you I could forever see
If this were the last time I could hear you
I would record your every word, so I could play it back a million
times
If this were the last time I could smell you
I would cut my nose off, so your smell would be the last
If this were the last time I could taste you
I would leave not a sting but a kiss
If this were the last time I could touch you
I would hold you in a long embrace, leaving the imagination to waste
If this were the last time....
I would simply tell you I love you and hope for the best

❖

Lie

You were always so good at lying
why don't you just keep on lying now?
Tell yourself that I still love you.
Tell yourself that my heart still belongs to you.
Lie to yourself,
It's the only way that your gonna feel
any affection from me anymore.
I have moved on to better things
to things you couldn't give me.
You want me to lie
and say that I still love you
but I just can't.
For four months I gave you
Nothing but the truth
and you always thought that I was lying.
Would you believe in me now?
Believe in this,
I don't have to lie when I say
I don't love you anymore.

J. Carlos Perez

Looks

I look at you, you look away, don't you see
That only goes to prove you still think of me
When I look at you, you look away
Averting eye contact that gives you away
Your eyes were always the ones to tell the truth
They were always the ones I sooth
You never could make them lie
No matter how hard you tried
I look away, you look at me,
I can still see you look at me

Lucky Charm

Wear me around your neck
like if I were a necklace
I'll be a lucky charm
protecting you from harm.

Wear me around your neck
and keep me in place.

Maybe, But No Thanks

I've spent so much time
Trying to make this work out
I forgot to think it through.

What if it isn't meant to be?
What if I deserve better
Than what you're giving me?

Maybe, but no thanks.

You are the queen of my heart.
You are the font to my text
And from you, It would kill me to be apart.

And right now, I'm truly dying.

J. Carlos Perez

Maybe You've Heard Of It?

I once knew this girl...
She was quite a sight to behold.
She had bright blue eyes
And long brown hair

She was smart and unique
Had her own way of doing things
Yet she had a tender heart
And that was her biggest flaw

She couldn't say no to anybody
or she would feel guilty all day
She moved off to California after we broke up
And I never saw her again
For five long years...

I saw her the other day...
I didn't even recognize her
She was the one who recognized me
I guess it was the way she looked

She no longer had those bright blue piercing eyes
In their place were dull lifeless blue eyes
Her hair was no longer luscious and silky
In fact it almost looked too white for her age

After we talked for a while I realized
That she had gone through many changes while she was gone
Many changes that I know she would not have done
If I had been there for her five years ago

She had opened her own business
Was making a fair amount of money
Maybe too much

Promise and Heartache

She had everything she ever wanted
And still had money left
That's where her trouble had been
Having too much

She began looking for things to do
Ways to spend that extra money that she had
Finding very few options to her appealing
But one sure did fit in quite well with her

It was methamphetamine
Maybe you've heard of it
Maybe you've heard of the stories it can do
Or maybe you yourself have tried it

I don't know about you
but after seeing my friend like that
I would be scared to even get near it

❖

J. Carlos Perez

My Dearest Friend

My Dearest Friend,
You have often told me,
That one-day I will be big and famous.
You tell me I can be anything that I want to be.

You tell me that one day
my talents will make me rich and wealthy.
To this I have one thing to say.

You, my dear friend, have the wrong idea of wealth.
I do not measure wealth in jewels and gold.
I don't even measure it with my state of health.

You see my dearest friend; I am already the richest man in the world.
I am the most fortunate man alive,
and it all comes down to one word.

My dearest "FRIEND"

I have everything I will ever need already.
I have caring parents, a lovable pet, most of all
YOU, my bestest friend.

❖

My Guardian Angel

In a world where
The good guy is in reality the bad guy
And where every medication can be abused.
I found you.

My Guardian Angel
That guides me through
The murky waters of the unknown.

You're always by my side
Even if you feel like your
Oh so far away.
Angels baby, they are everywhere and anywhere.

You are my Guardian Angel
That lives inside of my heart.
Everywhere and anywhere I go
You are there holding my hand,
Guiding my through the fog.

J. Carlos Perez

My Inspiration

Your beauty radiates
Like a thousand stars.
Illuminating my day
And driving away all
Temptation for anyone else.

You provoke every cell
In my head to inspiration.
Bringing out the best of
Words from their crypts
And onto paper for you.

If I could stay here
For another billion years.
I would want to spend them
Here next to you, hands together,
Dancing under the moons captivation.

Get up and leave your throne,
Leave your place from atop
The world and come with me.
Will make Angelina and Brad
Look like spots in or shadow.

You provoke every cell
In my head to inspiration.
Bringing out the best of
Words from their crypts
And onto paper for you.

72

Nightmares and Rainbows

Here I am again, another
Wasted dream on inconsistent
Memories. I can't believe I bother
To indulge myself in these reminiscent
Shadows of our past.

Nightmares and rainbows,
That's just the way shit goes.

The thought of you drowned out
By the taste of liquor, ravages
My mind, easing the need to shout,
Yet I've run out of places
To hide my broken heart.

Butterflies and pretty lies,
It didn't take long to realize.

You return, open arms, brand new heart,
Expecting me to fall right in.
Really you're just ready to tear me apart
Again, but honey, this is the fucking end.
Take you're pathetic love with you.

Nightmares and rainbows,
That's just the way shit goes.

J. Carlos Perez

Object X

I think of you minute after minute
Never stopping to think about anything else
You occupy my body and my heart
Leaving everything else a complete mess

When I think of you I loss track
Of time and my surroundings
I am completely lost with out you
And I am lost when I am with you

There is no escaping the way you make me feel
It follows...plagues me everywhere that I go
Is it a curse or a blessing
I confess sometimes I wish I hadn't meet you
That way I could live my life in peace

❖

Oceans Footsteps

I dig into the
Soft white sand
With my toes.

Flipping my hair
In the air
As gently it blows.

The ocean waves
Rhythmically and uniformly
Crash at my feet.

Clearing the footsteps
That my heart
Has left at every beat.

There used to be two pairs
But the waves, they have
Washed all but one.

J. Carlos Perez

Of Pain and Possibility

This morning I woke up--alone;
And had never felt better.
I made breakfast for myself
And sat down to eat--alone

During this time I was shown
Little love, other than that of
Family, so why is it some seek
A constant love to be shown?

I look at my friends and wonder
If they have a psychological NEED
To wake up to a different
Person every single day--I wonder...

If behind all the makeup, under
Their supposed perfect nature,
They satisfy themselves with a
Conditional love--a facade.

Are they incapable of feeling
The greatest of love, a true
Unconditional love which
Can be compared to no other feeling?

This of course, the love for oneself.

Tonight I'll probably sleep--alone
And I'll feel just fine.
I won't worry or fret the
Pain and possibility of forever being--alone.

❖

Oh, By the Way, I Took Your Coveralls Honey

I saw your cast iron mask
As you gently put it on
You looked so well
Until you put it on

Words of obscurity
Were spoken though that mask
Hiding how
You truly felt inside

How long could you
Truly keep this up?
How long could you
Keep on hiding?

J. Carlos Perez

One Final Time

I walk these halls
one final time.

Their long big corridors
don't seem so big anymore.

Not as big as when
I was a Freshman.

The people at this school,
they've changed every year.

But my friends
they've stayed the same.

I see my teachers,
one final time.

Some I loathe and
could care less about.

Yet others..
I will miss.

Friday June 6th
I'll walk on to the stage

One final time.

❖

One Perfect Line

The day I first met you
I searched everywhere
For one perfect line.

One perfect line
That would make me seem
Friendly and nice.

I settled for
"Hello my name's John."

The day I realized I loved you
I searched within me
For one perfect line.

One perfect line
That would express my love
Yet not be too over dramatic.

I kept it simple and said
"I love you"

The day I asked for your hand
I looked everywhere
For one perfect line.

One perfect line
That would get the message across
Yet not pressure you into an answer.

I knelt on my knee and said
"Will you marry me?"

Today again
I will search everywhere

J. Carlos Perez

For one perfect line.

One perfect line
That lets you know
Exactly how I feel tonight.

I think I'll settle for
"Goodbye, I don't love you anymore."

Past, Present, Future, The Moment

Yesterday,
I ran my fingers
Along the curvature
Of my steering wheel
Thinking how
Your body might feel
Under my lingering fingers.
Not knowing whether
The rekindled feelings for you
Were true or just
A side effect of
The drug you blew from your mouth.

Today,
I saw you
And couldn't help but stare,
Ignoring what anybody else
Thought or said.
What weird looks?
These,
I'm simply trying
To take you all in
But your beauty radiates
In such a way that it blinds.

Tomorrow,
I'll sit in agony
As I wonder how your day
Is going
And I'll worry myself to death,
Wondering whether you're okay.
Though I'm not usually a prayer,
I will do everything I can
As a preventative measure
Whether you're okay or not.

J. Carlos Perez

Next week,
You'll be gone
And things will go
Back,
To the way they were.
I'll be alone
And surrounded with self-loathing.
I'll think back to the
Short moments we shared
And wonder if
During any of them
You thought something of me.

In the next second,
I will finish figuring you out
And realize my first impression
Of you was way off,
I'll forget about the future
And live in the moment.

Then I'll wonder,
What at first did you think of me?

❖

Perception

Turn away
Your looks, they make me feel so...
Detached.

Hold your tongue
Your words, they penetrate my very....
Soul.

I can't bring myself
To forget all the things we went through.
They have been forever tattooed
In the chambers of my heart.

Keep your hands
To yourself.
Your touch
Like an icy breath,
Sends chills down my spine.

J. Carlos Perez

Psycho

I like this room
It's so quite and tranquil
There's no screaming and yelling
I can do what I want
And except for a few occasions
I'm practically alone

I hate this room
It's all yellow and fluffy
There's nobody here
It seems like a loony bin
What do they think I am?
A psycho or something

❖

Quantum Mechanics and Hydrodynamics

Uncertainty,
It's what we are living in today
I watch TV
And see guys like Michio Kaku
Talking about a infinite number of parallel universes
In which things differ from one to the other
And how in some, the laws of physics might not exist as we know
them
In another universe in the fourth dimension,
I have no hair
And in another I am a midget
I don't know of all the possibilities but,
One thing I know is that
In every one of those infinite universes
My love for you surpasses the amount of energy
Required to open a wormhole
(More commonly referred to as Planck Energy)
My love for you only gets stronger
From universe to universe
One thing I wonder though
Is if in any of those parallel universes
We are actually together
Loving each other
Like we were meant to be

J. Carlos Perez

Question

Don't ask me if I love you,
Because that question offends me,
If I could stack coin atop coin,
To make a tower out of all my feelings,
Believe me it would reach the sky

Even though you are away,
What I feel gets greater and greater,
Sometimes it scares me just to think,
Where am I going to put all this love
When it doesn't fit into my chest?

It wouldn't matter if you moved to another galaxy,
You would still be inside me,
Least to say that I live in a world inside of you

Because no matter how far you are,
No matter how many questions you ask,
It doesn't matter where you are,
Because you live here......in my heart

❖

Reach Out

Created by the elements
To be fragile and frail
You try to reach out
For help but fail.

Everyday deeper and deeper
You fall into a bottomless pit
Where it seems you wont be coming back.
Don't worry at the bottom a candle is lit.

As long as I'm here you'll
Always have someone
To guide you through the darkness.
I'll be a candle brighter than the sun.

All you have to do is reach
Our for my hand.
Have faith in yourself
And reach out to your friend.

J. Carlos Perez

Read This Shit When You're Feeling Ignored

Lately I've been noting but quiet,
Words kept in by the sorrow I've felt.
There's so much I've been dealt
That I wonder if things will be alright
Yet, the answer is always there
In front of me the whole time.
I love my friends and to be fair
I know I tend to place them outside of rhyme
But that's simply because I know
No way to let them know how
Much they help me in my woes.
If you're reading this now
I'm sorry I haven't given you
The attention you deserve.
Without my friends I truly don't know what I'd do,
Please set aside all insecurities and concerns
And think back to all the times we've shared
Take this time to swiftly adjourn
Your feelings of neglect, I've always cared

❖

Replication Complex

Remember when we were young
Our dreams and hopes floated in the air,
We built castles in the clouds
And watched the night-sky as the stars spelt out our names.

I miss the way we were back then...

When summers meant day long beach trips
And a day in the park was like an excursion in the jungle.
You were you and I was I There was no need to pretend
Yet thing changed and we both went on our way

I miss the way things were back then...

Seeing you in front of me, I can hardly breathe I can hardly speak
Part of me wants to say a childhood joke
But the self-conscious part holds me back
What after all these years did you think of me?

I miss the way we were back then.
You were you
And I was I,
There was no reason to pretend.

J. Carlos Perez

Room For You

Girl, there's something I've been
Meaning to tell you about.
Don't speak, just keep silent for
A minute while I get this all out.

You've had, such an influence on
Me these past few days.
It's hard for me to stop
Thinking about your gaze.

Those eyes, a perfect blend
Of brown melts me to the ground.

I've had, my mind on
You all day long.
And I didn't find a better
Way to say this than a song.

I've made a room for you in my heart

Yeah, I've made a room for you in my heart.

Said it All (The Next Guy)

I don't even know why
You have to try
When I can already tell by
That look in your eye
What you're going to say is a lie

Your eyes have said it all
They tell me of his call
They tell me you've moved on
To the next guy

The next guy isn't me
The next guy doesn't see
He's just a pawn in a game
And I curse you, Dame

But beware slug,
I now come equipped with salt

J. Carlos Perez

Saying Goodbye

Tonight I have to say goodbye.
I have to give up on all the fading memories
And the half present friendships.
I am tired and broken.
There is nothing else I can do to salvage this.

The butterflies and pretty lies
Have lost all beauty
I'm fooled no longer by your broken promises.

No, you can't take it back now
Those words have already slipped through your lips.

But tonight I'm having trouble saying goodbye
How can I when all I want is for you to stay?

Don't say a word
The silence keeps things safe for the moment

Scribbles

This is not a poem,
So lets just call it...
Scribbles

Scribbles that go down on paper
Some being scratched out
And others left to be read

Scribbles with no meaning
With no message behind them
Just a bunch of scribbles with no feelings

Scribbles that are unable
To tell you how
Exactly it is that I feel

J. Carlos Perez

September

Do you remember
Those warm nights in September;
Your late night whispering
In the wee hours of the morning
As a star filled sky above our heads
Played witness to our makeshift beds

I still remember
Those long nights in September;
Your hair flowing in the air
As we released our cares
And made fire in the sky,
Our lips parting in their last goodbye.

I still remember
Those nights in September
Tell me dear, do you remember?

Shadows (an Illusion)

Goodbye to hellos and hello to goodbyes
The end has come; I can see it in your eyes.
I knew this day would come with a tear
But that's not the only thing that I fear.
You. I might never see again
and I haven't yet found a place to begin.

I'm not ready to see you go away.
I'm not ready to have to think of you every day,
As a memory long forgotten in the past.
A shadow of an illusion that didn't last.
It bugs me to see that you take it so well.
Oh please do come and tell.
How you do it so well?
Is there no hope then? A horrid spell.

❖

Shambles

I am in shambles
And you are a tree.
Your branches have grown
To the deepest part of me.
Loosely we dance
In the dew of the morning.
Together we sink in
Our in-built self-loathing.

I am in shambles.

❖

J. Carlos Perez

She Wears Faith (between her breasts)

She wears faith between her breasts
A symbol which with her has lost all meaning.
Explain to me how you can be a
Christian when you're the spitting image of the devil?
She struts around,
A Christian model
Her two faces forcing sin
Down the throats of the young,
Forcing sin onto the innocent.
Her charming good looks
Are her weapon.
Her charming good looks
Are every boys demise.
She wears faith between her breasts.
She swears in Gods name
She is the victim
Yet uses the serpents tongue
To persuade her followers
Into believing her every lie
This woman has no friends
No, she only has slaves
Who believe they are cared for.
She wears faith between her breasts.

❖

Silent Screams

Over the fields
hear her screams.
Across the oceans
hear her screams.
Through the ground
hear her screams.
In the air
hear her screams.
Everywhere
hear her screams.

The Earth is screaming to be heard.
Can you hear the silent screaming
given off by the polluted air?

Can you hear the silent screams
the toxic water filled with waste yells?

Can you hear the silent screams
the Earth is yelling out at you?

My throat hurts from screaming
and I haven't said a word.

Imagine if we all heard the screams
and did what they say.
Would her beauty still be rotting,
crumbling as humanity procreates?

Imagine if we all changed one thing;
did one thing different for one week.

What if we all picked up "one" piece of trash,
would it make a difference?

J. Carlos Perez

Sketch

I draw every wrinkle
Every dimple
Your very soul,
I let not any
Feature go by
Undrawn,
Hour after hour
I slave
Perfecting the sketch,
Line after line
That soon become shapes
That become the mirror image of you

❖

Skips and Stops

Every time that I see her
My heart skips a beat and stops
She means the world to me...
I wished I could say the same for her

Love's a bitch
And so is not being able to know...
Know how the person you love feels
Or what that person thinks...skips and stops

I need her to know how I really feel
Without any pressure to decide about our future
If for just that one magical moment
It would just be us and no future....skips and stops

I guess its better this way...
Not knowing anything at all
Just wondering when my heart will
Finally skip and stop for the last time

Skip and stop...
Skip and stop...
Skip and stop...
Stop beating and die....

J. Carlos Perez

Somebody Like You

If I were a mad scientist
On a search for perfection,
I don't think I would have
Trouble making my creation.
I would make my Frankenstein
Something exactly like you.

If I were a musician
On a search for a classic,
I would tune up my guitar
And hand you the mic.
I would make my song sound
Something exactly like you.

If I were a director
On the search for a Grammy,
The writer would have to
Fir you in every shot to suit me
I would make sure the movie
Was all about you

Someone Like You

Never again will your smiles haunt me,
And never again will your eyes taunt me.
Never again will your voice give me chills,
And never again will you make me take those pills.
I wont love you.
I won't know you.
I won't even remember you.
I won't give you things
In hopes that they'll make you
Love me.
I won't look at the back of your head in
Algebra class
Hoping you'll catch me.

I won't ever love someone
Like you
Ever again.

J. Carlos Perez

Something Yet Nothing

I was going to write about something
But then I decided to write about nothing.
There is no way I can write a sestina when
I have trouble writing a poem as it is
Already. So here is my attempt at
Writing something about nothing interesting.

I thought it would be interesting
If I added a little bit about something
But that would be an attempt at
Writing something in place of nothing.
You see, the hardest thing is
Writing about something when
You have absolutely nothing to say and when
You know if you did, it wouldn't be interesting.
The difference between what you expected to read is
That you were expecting something
And in its place you got nothing.
I don't even know where the rhyme is at.

Oh, would you look at
That. No, you don't. You'll see the scheme when
You clear your mind and have nothing
Inside of it that's interesting.
Here, let me add something
To keep you reading. The answer to life is
Nothing. I wonder if this is
Enough to keep your mind at
Bay and realize this is actually about something.
I know it's hard to see when
You're used to reading interesting
Novels instead of sestinas about something yet nothing.

I just really have nothing
To say that you would consider is

Somewhat mind-boggling or interesting.
The good thing is that this is good at
Wasting your time when
You have nothing to do instead of something.

You'll never find anything interesting in reading sestinas about
nothing.

The thing about something, when you think about it, is
You don't wonder where it's at. It's plain as day. But with nothing
you have no questions like who? What? Where? When?

❖

J. Carlos Perez

Sonnet ACA 111

I was sitting in ACA one eleven,
When out of nowhere an angel appeared.
She had the sanctities of being from heaven.
And had great big wings with no bushy white beard.

I looked at her in a state of disbelief.
How was it that I was seeing such a being
Was it coming for me, a thief
Or was it all an illusion I was seeing.

I rubbed my eyes with a fury
And pinched myself on the leg
But her I still could see.
Then I looked down and saw her prosthetic peg.

Apparently she's no angel.
She's a hottie named Emily Pearsel

Spanish Is All The Rave And So Are You

Estoy atrapado en este mundo
En lo cual flores murmuran tu nombre
Y la luna me hace pensar en tus ojos.
El viento acaricia mi cuerpo
Y me recuerda a tus brazos.
Pensarías que estoy feliz
Pero en eso estoy en desacuerdo.
Todas esas cosas me asen ver la distancia
Y tú no estás aquí conmigo

I'm trapped in this world
In which the flowers murmur your name
And the moon makes me think of your eyes.
The wind caresses my body
And it reminds me of your arms.
You'd think I'd be happy
But with that I'm in disagreement .
All those things make me see the distance
And you're not here with me

J. Carlos Perez

Spanish Is Overrated and So Are You

Eres la luz de mi mañana.
La flor que me deslumbra.
Eres mi suspiro de aire fresco.
La única que adoro.

Muchos no logran tener a alguien
A quien lo cual puedan confiar completamente.
Pere en ti yo confió incondicionalmente.

Tu vos me deja sin aire con que respirar.
Por ti no hay nada que me pesaría dar.
Cuando estoy contigo me sumerjo
En agonía. Lejos de ti simple soy un despojo.

Pero tú no me tomas en cuenta.
Yo para ti soy un estorbo

Que es ese sabor en mi boca?
Oh si,
El aire fresco…
Está infectado con carcinógenos

You are the light of my mornings.
The flower which amazes me.
You are my breath of fresh air.
The only one I adore.

Many never come to have someone
Whom they can trust completely
But in you I trust unconditionally.

Your voice leaves me with no air to breath.
For you there's nothing I wouldn't give.

When I'm not with you I submerge
In agony. Away from you I am a fool.

But you don't take me into account.
I am but an obstacle in your way.

What's that taste in my mouth?
Oh yeah,
The fresh air...
It's tainted with carcinogens.

Spring

I don't know why I even try anymore
Spring, It will come never more.
Perhaps my winter hands repel it
Or perhaps in my life it sits unfit.

It's not as though I abhor
What Spring stands for.
I've tried my best to usher it in
Yet close and secret, like my soul, I stay within.

Springs cooing voice can be heard
When the winds of destiny are stirred.
But still I refrain.
I'd rather live with this unspoken pain.

Your voice,
Rejoice.
You're free.
Just let me be.

J. Carlos Perez

Swimming

I've been swimming in the thoughts
Of losing you, of
Never being able to see
Your big brown eyes
And honestly I can't help
But drown in those thoughts.
I'd rather die than go on
Living a full day without you.

Cordial Denial

There's no telling how much I've
Thought about you in the past few days
Wondering if I should call or not.
Am I coming off as desperate much?
I'm wondering what you think of me
Like what you think of my messy hair or
The fact that I'm pretty soft spoken

Steal My Data

You piss me off
To the point of
Hysteria.

Your deep inside
My system tearing
It all to shreds.

Your brutal attacks
Prevent me from doing
My work like writing.

I hope I can get rid of you
Or else I'm going to die.
Why wont you just leave.

Wait I know the solution
Here comes my friend
McAfee Virus Protection.

Man I hate computer viruses
Like you. All this from
Downloading a cracked game.

J. Carlos Perez

Thank You

You said goodbye, on a mid-summer morning,
Expecting me to fall in sorrow and pain,
But there were no words from me.
I simply turned and went on my way.
That's all I would do at that moment.
Words had escaped my mind and thoughts.

But now that I think about it,
I think I would have simply said:
"Thank You".
I needed to say thank you for all the
Things you ever did for me.
Even if it all ended with me
Going back to the same way I
Was in the Beginning, before I met you.

That Well Was Me

Ravished I was, that well was me
To see that sight that I did see
Stretched across the bosom of life lay she
Splendid and glorious, so full of glee
I am in love, that well is me

The Cube

The cube,
It torments.
A week and still no avail.
You would think that
A simple 3x3 cube would be easy,
Well guess what it's not.

I turn the fucker around,
I hit it against the floor
I get so made with it,
I throw it at the board.

Oh well I guess there's more detention.

Instead of doing work,
I'm working on this cube
Damn the man who came up
With this infernal device.
It's ruining my life
I can't go to sleep because of the stress.

Doesn't this toy come with instructions?
Oh wait they are still in the packaging,
I could have used them before
I lose my girlfriend and life.

J. Carlos Perez

The Dreamer

The smell of death, thick and sharp,
hangs mildly around the silhouette of a fatal dream.

A fragile dream made up of the most precious stones.

A kiss of rose glazes her cheeks as
guilt washes over her and she realizes, she took
deaths boney hand once more.

Just once is all they said it'd take.

Why she falls to old habits, she doesn't know.
She's gone over it one too many times in her head
and still it seems like the only escape she has.

Escape from the world.

The over zealous self conscience breaks down the attempts
of quitting, an unattainable feat for the dreamer.

The smell of death, thick and sharp,
hangs mildly around the silhouette of a fatal dream.
The smoke, hanging idly in front,
a mockery of all she's tried to overcome.

The dreamer fades away into the
shadows which engulfs her.
Afraid to take aid in the one true light in her life,
a light cast without self-gain, she recedes into
the unforgiving hands of death.

The Girl Who Got Away

You ask me how I will remember you
I reply that I will remember you
In both my heart and my brain
In my brain, your physical beauty resides
Though you may get old and gray
What you are now will always stay
Like a digital photograph
Clear and vivid it will remain
Your inner beauty resides in my heart
Where there is a special place
Because you have shown me your tender side
The very essence of you is in my heart
In my heart for eternity and a day
Though words may fail
I'll remember you to my dying day
Even though I'll be old and gray

❖

J. Carlos Perez

The Last Poem Ever

I watched her shaking with starlit eyes
As the cold winter breeze licked her body
And the darkness of the night devoured her presence.

A bitter taste arose in my word choked throat
As I walked towards her, hands beginning to water
Inside of my frozen dry pockets.

Her smile brighter with every step taken forward
And her eyes like emeralds reflecting the light from the heavens
That were eager to have her in their kingdom.

No pleasant salutations exchanged;
None being needed for the bitter aftermath
Would surely follow in mere seconds.

"This is the last poem ever"
I say with knife like words,
Stabbing her heart and twisting the handle.

I hand her a page torn from a notebook
Written on it a few thought out lines
Sure to cause pain in her life.

It reads:
"Forget you I can't, forget you I won't
You are forever seared in my heart for better or worse.
Your betrayal hurt me deeply but hate you I don't

Saying goodbye will not be easy
Nor will I be around to say it
My feelings for you make me queasy already.
Goodbye my love,
Goodbye my dearest friend"

The Only Thing That Matters

I'm not wanting to be mean
But sometimes I wish you'd cry
Not when your alone but when your next to me
Cry away all your sorrows on my left shoulder

That way I could wipe away all your tears
And let you know how much I care
I'd hold you there, like nothing else mattered
Because for me, you're the only thing that matters

So go ahead and think of me
Even if you're oh so far away
At least that way I know your thinking of me
And perhaps even shedding a tear

I'd hold you there, like nothing else mattered
Because for me, you're the only thing that matters

J. Carlos Perez

The Strong Can Still Crumble

You always thought I was the strong one.
 You always thought that I was holding you up.
Baby don't tell me your leaving, I fear that I will fall.
Don't you see neither of us were strong.
We were strong together,
But apart we will crumble

The Ultimate Price

Flesh is torn leaving behind a sickening gash
Nothing to live for death is coming at last
His eyes roll back, his mind going black
Now is when he wonders why did I come to Iraq
The answer is obvious no need to think twice
He is serving his nation, paying the Ultimate Price
He is there to protect those too cowardly to fight
Hiding in bushing and running in the cover of night
As he lay there dying he knows he did right
He protected freedom paying the Ultimate Price

The Things I Hate About You

The days go by
Relentless as they have
For what seems like an eternity now
Now that I've had time
To think things over
With the scrutiny that I
Usually do.
I realized how many things
About you I truly do hate.

I hate you for never taking time,
And I hate you for making me rhyme.
I hate that I can't read your eyes,
And I hate you won't help me fly.
I hate that I love to write,
And I hate that you can't read between the lines.
I hate that I've written 100 poems,
And I hate that 57 of those are about you.
I hate that I've known you for years,
And I hate that I've never once seen you shed tears.
I hate that you don't care,
And I hate that you don't share.
I hate that I don't know how to talk to you,
And I hate that you never learned to listen.
I hate that you ask for my opinion,
And I hate that you don't take it into consideration.
I hate that you ruined my life,
And I hate that you don't realize.
I hate that I've never said this to your face,
And I hate that you never once asked.
I hate that I write stupid poems to tell people how I feel,
And I hate that I can't say it to their face.
But mostly, I hate that you wont even understand that,
This is all about you.

❖

117

J. Carlos Perez

There's Nothing Else

There is nothing else I've been
Looking forward too
More than this conversation,
Been looking forward to
Telling you of the connection
I've felt for you.
The way your complexion,
Though you're eyes aren't blue,
Drives me into desperation
At not being able to
Express my affection
Towards you.

This platonic love
I've been harboring inside me
Has risen above
The limits of safety.

There is nothing else I've been
Looking forward too
More than the moment of confession
When I tell you I love you

❖

Things To Do

I sit in solitude
Staring off into
Pictures of you and me.

Thinking....
Reminiscing
Of the way things used to be.

I feel like I took
Everything you ever gave me
For granted.

Your trust, your friendship
I took it all and
Left hurt, pain implanted.

All I can do now
Is stare off into
Pictures of you.

Hope, faith
Remembrance...
That's the only thing left to do.

J. Carlos Perez

This Feeling

There is something about you that has me reeling,
I don' know what it is,
But I can say that I am loving this feeling.

The way you look at me,
The way that you are,
There is nowhere else I would rather be.

This Is Not The End

Till the bitter end,
I will sit here telling you.
How much I loved you,
And how much I'll miss you.

This is not the end...

The last thing I want to do
Before the end comes for us.
Is cry there next to you.
Oh baby please don't fuss.

This is not the end....

Tides

I silently watched as your innocence
Faded away into the rising tide
Each wave clash taking some of your mask
Leaving with you no place to hide.

You scrambled for cover behind
Face less lies to no avail.
I could see right though them,
Through the gray and misty veil.

Behind your tough exterior
I see the fragile girl I once loved
The one who didn't care what others said
All she wanted was to be loved

J. Carlos Perez

Timewave Zero

Timewave Zero
Or Galactic Alignment
I still don't know exactly
Which theory I want to buy into
But I do know it doesn't matter.
Both theory's call for end of world events.
Whether they come to pass,
I don't know either.
It's all a big mess
I don't want to try to figure out anymore.
Mayans, Nostradamus, just whatever
Let us figure it out when the time comes.
What I do know,
Is that I love my family and friends.
Those I've known all my life
And those I just met.
No matter if the world ends
Or if it continues on its path of corruption,
I will know I loved you,
And I always will.
If December 21, 2012
Decides to take my life,
I will die with no regrets
For I had you in my life.

Tonight

I'll throw away all your things
On my way home tonight
I know I'll be doing wrong
Yet nothings ever felt so right

It's time I let go
It's time I learnt how to live
You've been holding me back
And right now it's time for me to give
The world back what it's dealt to me

And maybe I should have spent
Just a little more time with you
But then again what would have been the use
With people like you there's nothing you can do
To make them comprehend
To make them realize

I loved you more than
I ever let you know
But all that's behind me
I don't love you anymo'

I finally figured out,
Who you truly are
And honestly,
This wouldn't have gotten far

I've got so many things,
I'd like for you to see
I told you I'd be going big
And quitting just not me
When you see me in the paper
Please don't hesitate to call
I'll be the first one at your doorstep

J. Carlos Perez

When you've lost it all

Because honestly,
You've got nothing going for you at all.
❖

Two and Two

I've been wondering what you think of me
Do you look at me and see what I see
Messy hair, and blood shot eyes
And put two and two together
Do you think of me as a stupid kid
Living life yet throwing it away
❖

Truth Ridden Eyes

As your eyes began to water,
Your tears turn into liquid graphite.
Simmering down your cheeks they go,
Writing my name as they fall.
You may say that it's not me
But your eyes tell it all.

Twitter Sized Poem

Call this a reminder,
An annoyance in your hinder.
Or call it as you know'em.
A Twitter sized poem.

J. Carlos Perez

Unconditional Love

Have you ever heard of
Unconditional love?

Loving someone regardless
Of what they may
Or may not do.

I was once a believer
Of this so called
Unconditional love.

But now,
I don't know
What to believe in.

Your promises
They meant nothing
To you.
You broke them
And along the way,
You broke me.

So take your petty
Sorrow and your
"We can still be friends"

I don't want to see you
I don't want to hear you
If at all possible
I don't want to remember you.

❖

Untitled 2

"Why should I play the Roman fool?"
I who treated you like life itself
Pampered you with gifts and jewels
I shall not bring this spectacle of a love
To an abrupt end by my own hand
There will be no blood of my own
Shed by my very sword
You speak'st of love and honor
Yet you were the thorn from
The most beautiful rose, that
Struck my heart and took it to the grave

❖

J. Carlos Perez

Untitled 3

I don't remember
Seeing
Breathing
Living
Next to anyone
As beautiful
As you.

You have literally
Fixed
Patched
Changed
My life
In a way that
Nobody has.

I want to
Sink
Soak
Die
In the
Essence of
You.

One of these days I'm gonna
Run
Jump
Fly
Out to you
And take
You away.

We will live
Joyfully
Peacefully

Happily
Ever after
In a world
Were only we exist.

Villanelle for a Dearest Friend

I know someone I'll love till the end
Bright blue eyes and pale white skin;
My dearest friend

She's one of the only people on whom I can depend
And I hold her friendship deep within.
I know someone I'll love till the end

When we have problems, our friendship we mend
So close it feels as if we're of kin.
My dearest friend

Our distance now is hard to comprehend
But I know close we are and have been.
I know someone I'll love till the end

Possible, a letter to write and send
But where to begin?
My dearest friend

A year's time it took for me my trust extend
To someone I feel now is as close to me as a twin.
I know someone I'll love till the end
My dearest friend

J. Carlos Perez

Villanelle For A Loved One

Every day I think about you
And I further realize
No one shines as bright as you.

It's the way you do everything that you do
And the gleam in your eye.
Every day I think about you.

And it's the way I get the blues
Every time we say our goodbyes.
No one shines as bright as you.

And yes, it's true,
I'll love you until the day I die.
Every day I think about you.

There's nothing I wouldn't do
To keep you in your state of natural high.
No one shines as bright as you.

I don't know what I'd do without you
And that's why when you're not around
I think about you.
No one shines as bright as you.

Watching You Go

Your laugh is wearing thin
The callous hand of our love
Has begun to slowly let go.
Lets try to remember the days
When we learned to open
Each other's mouths, the days
When we learned the meaning
Of love.
If ever two have been one
I swear it was with you
Your laugh is wearing thin
Your brightness shines dim
The pain you are feeling breaks
Me, it breaks me knowing
There is nothing I can do. I
Can do nothing but watch you go.

❖

J. Carlos Perez

Waiting

"I'll wait for you"
You said one day
Forty years 3 days ago
On a hot summer day
Here I am
A weathered fool
Sitting below our tree
Still waiting for you

When I'm Gone

I fight the urge to cry
All things must soon die
There's no need to obsess
Lest love we should value less

When you see me walk away
They'll be nothing you can do but pray
Cuz you're going to miss me when I am gone

Waking Up (to find all your friends are gone)

I wake up, it seems
Every night from dreams
Into a nightmare.
I'm all alone
All my friends 've gone.
They used to call
But that happened less and less
Until not even a text to say
Hey!
Was spared in their time.
We kept in touch
Only because of my ...
Persistence?
No,
Only because of my fear
Of letting go of what I've known.
But then that too,
Wasn't enough

One day you too will wake up and find
That all your friends have left you behind.
But if you're smart,
You'll do like me.
Reposition your pillow,
Shed a few tears,
Star up at the ceiling,
Count the years
They've been gone,
And go back to sleep
Where they still exist,
Thinking of a few words
You wished you'd said to them.
"I will never forget you dear friends"
❖

J. Carlos Perez

What's A Promise Worth To You

Everything I do
Reminds me of the way,
The way we used to play
In the rain all day.

Baby I still think of you

What's a promise worth to you?
Do you really mean what you say?
Or is it just another thing you do
To break me down in every way?

You Do.

What's a promise worth to you?
Nothing, I can tell.
I can tell by the way
You left me on that day.
You left me playing alone on that day
What's a promise worth to you?

Don't apologize to me
Apologize to the feelings that you broke
You broke them all.

When We're Together

When we're together I drift away
On the clouds of the words you say.
They way you talk, laugh and the way you smile
Drives me crazy but all the while,
Soothes me down to a perfect bliss.

When we're together I feel warmth renewed,
Even with just the thought of you.
When I see you, I'm at a loss for air
And with you I just want to stay

As far as I know you could be somebody else's, boo
But I can't stop looking at you.
I want to hold you in my arms and keep you there
Because you're the only one who can make my day.

It's the way you have a way of saying hey
And the way our love is like a Shakespearean play.
Mysterious and tragic with an interesting end
So hush now and come take my hand.
When we're together I know the true meaning of love
That look in your eye makes me realize all that matters

J. Carlos Perez

When You're Gone

This feeling in my stomach,
It's so new,
I've never felt it before,
It's not love,
That I already feel,
It is something else,

What could it be?

It's hard to explain,
It's like an emptiness
That never gets fuller.
It's like a part of me is missing
Amputated without sedation.

This is how I feel when you're gone.

Where Has My Heart Gone

The pain grows unbearable
With each passing day
With each passing second
The pain is tremendous
It hurts just to reminisce
 I grab at my chest
There's no beat
Where has my heart gone?
Shouldn't I be dead?
The pain of the hollow cavity
Follows me around everywhere I go
The constant felling of emptiness
Emptiness that hurts and burns
 I grab at my chest
There is no beat
Where has my heart gone?
Perhaps I don't need it no more
Perhaps I have gotten used
To living without a heart
Perhaps after months of living without it
With my heart being in someone else's hand
My body has gotten used to the feeling of complete emptiness
Then why the pain?

❖

J. Carlos Perez

Where The Hell's Your Hope?

And what about my heart
Does it mean nothing to you?
So we should just move on and pretend
There was nothing we could do?
In a perfect world
This would all make sense
But not tonight, no not tonight.
It's been so long since
I gave up and I'm not planning to
I'm not content with losing you
I'm not going to let this go
You know I'd rather die.
So where the hells your hope
And why can't we just try?

❖

Who Would've Known

Who would've known
That behind those beautiful eyes
Could lay so much hate

Who would've known
That those wonderful feelings
Were just imitated...Fake

Who would've known

❖

Winter Speaks Of

Winter speaks of
Drawn out goodbyes and never-ending hellos

Winter speaks of
Warm mornings and serene conversations

Winter speaks of
A loss of breath and no words to say

Winter speaks of
Friendly hugs and make believe thoughts

Winter speaks of
Awkward silences in which I don't know what to say

Winter speaks of
Holding hands by using the smallest excuses to touch

Winter speaks of
A girl's body only to the likes of Aphrodite

Winter speaks of
A start of something new

Winter speaks of
You

J. Carlos Perez

Winters Due

It's one hundred and three degrees.
It's cloudy out, but there's no breeze.
The summer air smells of winters due
And I think of you.

Winters Inability To Let Go

Like a melody from the heart
Your words plays over in my head.
Falling like snowflakes in the summer
Scarce but ever blinding.

A blizzard once feared
I have come to accept
Your snippets of conversation
For what they are really are.

Winters inability to let go

xCousinx

Dear friend of mine,
I know they say the passage of time
Will make even the greatest of friends loosen their ties
But I say to you
We've both got eyes
Our friendship is clearly
Greater than that
In fact
I've welcomed you into my family
Dear cousin of mine
If ever your sad or feeling blue
Just think if me or this poem
I'll be there for you

❖

J. Carlos Perez

Yeah, I'll Always Feel The Same About You

Tonight as I watched you walk my way
I knew everything would be okay
For I saw the future in your eyes
And I saw, yeah, we would get on by

You reached and wrapped me in your arms
And I knew I'd be kept from harm
For only there have I felt secure
We were meant to be, yeah, of that I'm sure

Tonight I didn't want to go home
Even knowing you Id talk to on the phone
For your voice would only make me miss you more
It's true, yeah, that I swore

It's been a year but I remember it like last night
I know you've moved on now, through the light
For your soul was brighter than a Jupitarian day
And I know, yeah, it was meant to be this way

Even after death I know
My feelings for you are the same even if its harder to show.
For I'm still with my lover even through death and sorrow
I'll see you again someday, yeah, next year if not tomorrow

❖

You

I love you with every fiber of my being
Right now, your smile is all I'm seeing.
To be without you for any given time
Drives me into despair without a reason or a rhyme.
How do I get through each barbaric day
Without our kiss, your hugs, your touch, and the things you say.
My many thoughts of you consume me,
Without you, my joys and my senses reel
Never before have I let anyone my heart to steal
I would do anything for you
Life has meaning now and happiness renewed
Because of the way you look at me and act so kind.
Because I love you and your heart is mine.

J. Carlos Perez

You Do

I never meant to hurt you
And I know I hurt you bad
I am sorry for my mistakes
I am sorry for my faults

It's easy to say you're sorry
When you do not mean it
But you have to know the sorrow I am feeling
Hurts me as much as I hurt you

With eyes wide, open
I see you
With eyes shut
I see you

I cannot forget you
I know you cannot forget me either

Do not tell me you do not miss me
Cuz I see it in your eyes
You Do

You Know

Girl I know, there's a lot of things
You need to worry about.
Like what you're going to do
When you leave this town,
But the one thing I never
Want you to frown
About is what you're going to
Do when everybody casts you out.

Because you know,
I'll always be here,
You'll always have me
To fall back upon.
Girl I know, sometimes you feel
Like you've lost it all,
You feel like you've got nothing left
In your life.
But as long as I am here
I never want to see you shed a tear.
Just the thought consumes me,
The thought tears me apart.

Because you know,
I'll always be here,
You'll always have me
To fall back upon.

J. Carlos Perez

You Said (forever)

Do not repeat yourself,
I heard what you said.
I don't want you to feel sorry,
I loved what you said.
Your words,
Like honeycomb sweetness
Flowed through the air savored by all and
Known by so few.
It would only be fair
If I admit to my weakness
For if I were
More of a man, winters due
Would not be at hand.
Your melodic words,
Like harps playing in tune
With the midsummer air
Reached all parts of my heart,
A place known by so few.
I'll admit to my share
Of all of this. If I had been there,
If I had been there for you
We wouldn't be at this end.
I loved what you said,
When you said it to me.

❖

You Too

Every morning I wake
Up, knowing I have something
To live for, something to take
Me away
From my horrible day.

Every morning I know there is nothing
Anyone could ever say
To make me stop loving
Everything that makes you
You or the things that you do.

Every morning and every day
I think of a way to tell you
I love you in every possible way
A person could love another
Without becoming a bother.

I know you love me and I love you too.

J. Carlos Perez

Young Again

Who said
Boys can't be men and
Men can't be boys?
I remember being seven and
Not being able to wait still 18.
I remember
Always wanting to be able to smoke
And
Being able to cruise around in a brand new car.
Now that
I'm so close to being 18
And
Finally getting to do all the things I wanted,
I just
Want to be young again
And
Be able to stay home all day watching cartoons.
I'm not
Saying I'm a coward
And
Can't handle the responsibilities of a man.
I just
Wish I'd spent life slower
And
Done more things as a kid that I didn't get to do.

Short-Stories

❖

J. Carlos Perez

Adam Brindle

Adam Brindle sits
On a wooden bench,
Legs crossed
In front of him,
Sucking on the sweet heaven
He calls menthol cigs.

I watch him from
Across the street,
Inside a local shop,
Hiding from his gaze.

-His eyes a crystal,
Diamond like blue-

I've always been fascinated
By Adam Brindle.
His eccentricities
Keep me guessing
As to what he really is.

After minutes of watching
Adam Brindle
I'm convinced he plans
On sitting there forever.
The bus has come and
Gone many times but
Adam Brindle moves not a muscle.
He simply sits,
Staring forward
Sucking on his sweet heaven.

Finally, I step outside and
Walk over to where Adam

151

J. Carlos Perez

Brindle is smoking his
Fourth cigarette.
He smiles at me,
Perfect white teeth,
And says
"I've been waiting for you."

Flat and monotonous
His words hit me sharply,
I can feel his eyes on
Me,
Taunting a red wave
To wash over my face.
I begin to feel a bead of
Sweat forming on my forehead
As I begin to back step
But am stopped cold by
Adam Brindle
"Come on now,
You've been watching me for
Over an hour, you must sit
And talk.
Ask,
Ask as many questions as you want."

My first instinct is to run,
Run away,
From this man.

Yet, I don't follow my instinct,
Instead I sit. Obediently
I take a seat
Next to the statue like man,
Thinking I'm safe out in public.

Wasting little time
I quickly indulge in my questioning.

I ask Adam Brindle how old he is.
"28" He says flatly.
I look at him and his attire,
Noticing he is nicely dressed I ask,
"Why are you so dressed up for?"
He smiles a coy grin and answers,
"I just came from seeing a dead friend."
Intrigued by his lack of sadness
I ask,
"Did you not like your friend?"
Again he smiles,
Showing off his perfect white teeth.
"Of course I liked my friend,
I loved my friend."
I look into Adam Brindles
Crystal clear eyes and ask
"What happened to your friend?"
This time he frowns
Ever so slightly
But then again smiles.
"I got tired of the nagging,
So I killed my friend."

Clearly the man was lying,
Right?
He wasn't just going to admit
This so calmly to me,
Would he?

"How long ago did this happen?"
He takes a long draw from his
Menthol cigarette
And answers, coyly,
"About two hours ago."
At this point
Adam Brindle
Turned towards me and

J. Carlos Perez

Mockingly smiled his perfect
White teeth.
I knew he had to be kidding
There was no way this man
Had just killed someone.
Adam Brindle's
Countenance was calm
He wasn't worried about a thing.
No way he'd just killed someone
And was lazily sitting on a bench
Telling me of his deed.

Convinced he was lying
I continued further.
"What was your friend doing?"
Flatly he answers
"My friend kept telling me
To get up and get them
A drink.
I was trying to watch a game
Of basketball and hate
Interruptions."

I busted out in laughter
The excuse he had just given
Convinced me fully he was kidding.
Aside from being creepy,
Adam Brindle
Had a very active imagination.

Too entertained to end his game
I asked,
"So you're running way
Before the
Cops
Find you?"

"No.
Actually I'm going to the groceries
To pick up some milk for
My cat.
The police,
They'll never catch me.
Adam Brindle brings his feet under
Him from their crossed position
And throws his cigarette on the floor.
He turns towards me and asks
"Do you think I should run away?"

I think about it for a second and answer
"Well assuming you did kill
Your friend,
I'd say yes. You should,
Run away,
As far as you can.
Get away before anyone catches on
To what you did."

"Do you think I could get away?"
He asks.

"Yes.
If you tried hard enough I think
You could get away with it."

"What about you?
You know I did it.
Wouldn't you give me up?"

"I would probably
Think about doing it
But the fear of you returning
To kill me
Would surely put me off

J. Carlos Perez

From telling anyone."
I admit to
Adam Brindle.

"Though I probably could get away
With it as you've said,
Could I get away from myself?
I know what I did
And will never be able to forget it.
I loved my friend.
If I ran away
This secret would run away
With me."

"I suppose you're right,
But if you're so worried about your
Conscience
How were you able to just
Kill
Your friend you loved?"

"Sometimes we must do things
We don't want to
But for the better of humanity
We must."

Adam Brindle
Watches as the bus
Rounds the corner and pulls up to the bench.
Slowly he stands erect,
Directs his gaze to me and says
"The body is in a trunk in my closet.
I cut the body up and vacuum sealed it
In small parts."

Adam Brindle smiles his
Perfect white teeth

And then gets on the bus.

I watch the bus until
It's gone in the horizon
And then continue my day
Like nothing happened.

❖

Bartender
*Co-Authored with Jason Shores

Driving home from work, Aaron contemplated suicide. His despair was dark and heart wrenching as if someone were trying to tear out his heart. As his foot pressed harder on the pedal he thought about how easy it would be to not let go and simply drive off into the welcoming hands of the darkened woods around him. It would feel so much better if he could just cease to exist. The lure of oblivion called to him as he considered the emptiness he felt inside. "Nobody I care about would even notice I am gone," he kept telling himself, trying to convince himself to do it. "Everybody I care about is gone. I am all alone abandoned. What will they care?" The harmonious music playing hummed alongside the roar of the engine as the car speed up faster uphill. Within 100 feet from the incline a sharp turn waited for Aaron along with a steep drop into trees; of course, Aaron knew this.

"There's no shame in giving up," thought Aaron in an internal monologue as if the devil and God were raging inside of him. "It would be so much easier if I could just end it all right now." Then he thought: "But if you do it, think about all the people you'll be letting down. Even if you don't care about those people, they care about you. Do you want them to feel what you're feeling right now?" As he thought of this, another wave of desperation seemed to flow through his psyche making it feel as if there was a great weight on his chest making it difficult to breathe. The steering wheel, moist from sweat, vibrated softly beneath Aaron's hands. Adrenaline pulsed in his body. Every noise and vibration echoed in his ears. He could hear the scraping, grinding roar of the tires making contact with the asphalt as he raced uphill.

Around him he could hear a soft murmur of voices faint but clear to him. "You know she's not worth it. 'I'm not going to say there are other fish in the sea and I am not going to bombard you with clichés but I will say, It's not the end of the world.'" Through the fog of emptiness, Aaron knew the voices were right. Even if they had used a quote from a song to make their point, the voices were right. Nobody is worth taking your own life for. It'd been foolish for him to think so. He backed his foot off of the pedal and slowly pressed down on the brake. Instead of hearing the screech of his worn brakes, he heard nothing. His heart skipped a beat as he realized the brakes were not working. Now, at the top of the incline, Aaron saw a car stopped in the road in front of him. Too close to do anything about it, He tried to swerve over to the other lane but it wasn't enough. The screech of tires penetrated the silence of the night. The sparks were the first thing he saw as they became a raining golden haze all around him in the too fast chaos of the moment. He could tell he was upside down, his car sliding down the road , perhaps in to oblivion. The only thing Aaron could do was cover his face with his arms and hope the car came to a stop soon before hitting another object or worse, falling off the edge of the drop. This one singular moment seemed to stretch out forever, the fear, and pulsing adrenaline in his system pulling a handful of seconds into an eternity.

Finally the car stopped, and the sensation of violent jerking movement ended. Aaron could hear the music playing and thought everything was all right. If the music was still playing it couldn't have been that bad, right? He slowly unlatched the seatbelt from its fastener, holding himself up with a freehand so he wouldn't fall onto the roof. Gradually he worked himself down and crawled out the broken window. Aaron stood up and looked around him. His car was a mess. Worse than he'd thought. The front end was bare bones metal, the engine exposed to the air by a large missing chunk of the cars exterior. Debris lay scattered around him in a plethora of metal and glass like someone had lain all the pieces out on the road for inspection and then littered it all with a coating of crystalline dust. Faint but pungent, he smelled the gas before he even saw it. He backed away and looked at the other car and tried to discern a human body inside through the window but couldn't tell if anybody was still in there. "Maybe there wasn't anybody in there. Maybe it died on them and they just left it there?" Anything would have been better than what Aaron saw as he approached.
Aarons trepidation grew as he neared the other car once again feeling despair at his situation. He heard the other person before he actually saw him. A soft wail coming from beneath the chassis of the vehicle

159

made him jump back in surprise. Quickly he threw himself on the floor and saw the other man, blood covered and broken. "What have I done? Fuck, what have I done?" Aaron paced around trying to figure out what to do. He couldn't just leave the man to die. Yet he also didn't want to go to jail. Surely they would throw him in jail for this. "His family, they'll surely sue." Without thinking any more, Aaron reached into him pocket and pulled out his cellphone. He dialed 911 and then quickly told them about the man under the car and left. With no car of to drive off on, Aaron ran into the welcoming outstretched arms of the woods. As he ran he wrestled the battery compartment off of his phone and threw it out. A little while after throwing the battery away, he threw the SIM card out and then finally the phone itself a while later. Aaron ran and ran until he felt he couldn't any more and still a little more. "If I get caught now there will be nothing to help me he thought. I ran. I'm a fucking criminal. God I didn't mean to kill the man."

There came a point when Aaron thought he heard dogs barking in the distance, thought they were police dogs and climbed a tree thinking it to be the best place to hide. His heavy breathing slowly became a dry rasping sound escaping from his throat uncontrollably. When Aaron finally convinced himself he had imagined the dogs barking, he climbed down from the tree and cunningly made his way towards the outer edge of the woods. In the distance he could see the glowing aura of city lights.

Slightly cocky about his situation, Aaron walked out of the woods and across the road to what appeared to be a bar. A neon sign outside flickered on and off, no doubt neglect by the patron. In bright pink letters in read: Jordan's Bar and Grill. Seeing no cars in the parking lot, Aaron walked in without thinking twice.

The aroma of beer was pungent. Like a dark veil, cigarette smoke hung in the air. At least, in Aaron's mind, it was what he'd always envisioned a bar to be. Contrary to his expectations, the inside smelled of pinewood cleaner and fries. The tables were clean and emitted a soft aura of a reflection due to the bright overhead lights. He walked towards the bar stools and sat down at the furthest one down from the door. He laid his head down on top of his arm and closed his eyes while he waited for someone to come out. "Where is everyone?" he thought as he tried to take deep breaths to regain some semblance of control.

At the sound of heels clicking on the porcelain white floor, Aaron raised his head and saw a early 20's woman staring at him from the other site of the counter. "I'm sorry but we're closed. I must have forgot to lock the door." Aaron simply stared back at her. "Did you not hear me? We are closed."

"I…I…did hear you. I just…uh… has anybody told you there is a strong similarity between you and Jessica Biel?"

"I can't say they have. Should they have?" questioned the undoubtedly attractive bartender.

"Well the similarity is there, you could pass off as her twin."

"I guess that's your way of telling me I look good, comparing me with another woman. Too bad I don't know who that is."

"Really? You've never seen Blade Trinity or The A-Team?"

"Can't say that I have but like I said, we're closed and I would really appreciate it if you left. I might not look strong but trust me, I've had my share abusive men who needed to be dealt with a little force."

"I'm not going to hurt you. I just want a little drink."

"Of course you do, why else would you be here at 3 in the morning. Of course you don't want a cheeseburger or fries. You want beer. Isn't that a surprise?"

"You don't know me. You can't judge me without even knowing a thing about me."

"Listen, one drink okay. But that's it. After that you leave."

"Okay, that's all I want. One drink."

The bartender stared at him for a minute expecting Aaron to tell her what he wanted to drink but never having drunk before; Aaron didn't know what to ask for. "So you going to order something?"

"Well, the thing is…I've never drunk before."

"Oh so let me guess, girl broke your heart and you're looking for an easy escape from the pain?"

"Uh…yeah pretty much. But how did you…"

"I can read it all over you. I'm good at doing that. I can also tell you aren't going to be quick about this. So let me lock the door so no more heartbroken fools walk in out of nowhere. I'm doing this only because I'm a sucker for other peoples stories and am pretty interested in yours."

"Okay, whatever, I just want something to drink."

"No, you want something to forget, and I'll drink to that." She said as she gracefully walked to the door and locked it. Aaron noticed that as she moved it was with a feline grace that suggested hidden power and strength. "I've had my personal share of hardship and know what it's like to want to forget." Aaron watched her as she went about setting out glasses for their drinks, her movements confident, sure, and full of a languid grace. She pulled the clean glasses from behind the counter, filling them up with a thick rich blend of beer.

"I also killed a man." Said Aaron in a tiny voice full of sorrow as his throat nearly closed before he could get the words out.

"What?" Asked the bartender in a surprised yet calm voice.

"I killed a man. Before I came here I got into an accident and killed a man."

"You're kidding right?"

"Nope. I hit a man's car and left him to die." Once again Aarons throat nearly closed on the words as the full impact of what he'd actually done began to sink in.

"You don't know he was dead. He might have survived. Can't always think so negative." Said the woman in a placating tone of voice.

"I'm pretty sure. Aaron said thinking of what his future might hold if he went to prison.

"Goddamn, your life really is fucked right now isn't it?" The woman said with a blank face, neither sympathetic, nor mocking.

"That's one way to say it, yeah." Said Aaron while he thought maybe the woman was mocking him

"We'll I already served us some drinks and don't really see you as a psycho killer. How about you go ahead and tell me about your day. What left you such a mess?" She said staring him in the eyes until Aaron dropped his own gaze.

"I don't know. I normally don't go around telling strangers my life story."

"My name is Janelle if that makes you think of me as less of a stranger. Besides, I doubt you normally go around almost killing people everyday either. Today will be a day of firsts."

"Okay." Said Aaron blinking in the face of her candor.

"So about this girl…" Janelle prompted him.

"Her name is Sarah Jane Williams, and she was my everything. I first met her when my family moved down from Maryland. For the first three years she made fun of me and bullied me. At the start of high school she went through some changes and we got closer. Ever since then she has been there for me when nobody else has."

"Ah, so you guys have a history together then. Tell me about her though, before you go on, I want to have a mental picture of who you're talking about." Said Janelle

"Well the most distinct feature about her, something I love, is her central heterochromatic eyes." Said Aaron, warming to his story now that there was someone to listen.

"Wow, hold on a minute. I don't know what that even means." Said Janelle as she looked at him quizzically.

"It means her eyes are different colors." Explained Aaron.

"Oh, so one is brown and one green. Something like that?" She asked leaning slightly forward interested in his answer. "No. They are both the same color. In that the center of them are blue and towards the outside they fade into a green color."

"Oh okay. I think I understand now." Said Janelle once again making eye contact with an unsettling directness that made Aaron a little uneasy.

"Her smile…is unlike any other smile I've ever seen. Just seeing it brightens my day. Or at least it did."

"What happened?"

"I don't really know. Everything had been fine the entire day. She simply called me after she got off work and told me to basically fuck off, never wanted to see me again." With that memory Aaron once again remembered perfectly that moment when he heard the words come from her mouth only to feel like his heart had been torn from his chest.

"Then what?" Janelle asked pulling him from his reverie.

"I felt like the world had been torn from me. Everything I cared about ripped away from my grasp."

"You didn't go to her and try to work things out?" Janelle asked

"Uh, no not really. I'm an emotional guy and get carried away sometimes."

"So all is not lost, yet?" She prodded

"Well if you put it that way, no. I guess she could be talked to and I don't know, convinced." Said Aaron, wondering if it was really possible.

"Well your story isn't as interesting as I thought it would be. Melodramatic bullshit if you ask me. Acting like a high school jock getting dumped for the first time." Said Janelle with just a slight hint of cold in her till now warm velvety voice.

"Hey! I thought we weren't going to judge." Said Aaron feeling confused, and a little hurt.

"I'm just speaking the truth. The only thing interesting you even said was you killing a man. How'd that feel. Did you feel powerful?" Asked Janelle as she looked at him once again with that direct and intense gaze.

"I didn't mean too! I told you it was an accident." Aarons voice had raised several decibels slightly above a light scream. Once again he was seeing in his mind the sparks that seemed to envelope everything in existence as he flew down the highway upside down hoping to survive.

"I'll tell you what, it's not power. When you kill a man the thing that feels the best is the control. The fact of knowing you control whether they live or die. As you hold them in your hands power does come to mind but it's the control that gets me." Janelle said with a glint in her eye, and a note of chilling cold in her voice.

"What the hell are you talking about?!" Asked Aaron now wondering if the woman was crazy.

"Come here. I want to show you something." The bartender stood up from her stool and gently grabbed Aarons arm.. "It'll only take a second and then you can come back to your drink." Led by a two-finger embrace, Aaron followed the voluptuous woman while he felt a growing apprehension that maybe telling her about the car wreck hadn't been the best Idea, especially if she was unstable.

"What are you going to show me?" He asked

"Don't worry about it. You'll see in due time. Just know, I am going to be you're first real heartbreak." She stated without a hint of irony, and as serious as if she were telling him the color of his eyes.

"My what?" He spluttered now completely confused.
Janelle turned around and placed her hands around Aarons face with surprising strength. She caressed his face and his messy hair. She got closer and pressed her lips against his still unmovable own. "I said I'm going to be your next heartbreak." She whispered in his ear.
As Aaron pulled himself away from her, he felt the sharp pain of a knife puncturing his upper abdomen and sliding up into his chest. His eyes opened wide, fear taking over his face. "What....why?" he managed to cough up confused as to what was happening, thinking that this couldn't be real. He must still be in the car hanging upside down. Surely any moment now he would awaken and find that he had somehow injured his chest in the accident. But oh how it hurt, there was a fire burning at the heart of him.

"I told you. Tonight is a night of firsts; your first real heartbreak, your first true taste of pain. Too bad this isn't my first time or it would have really been a night of firsts." Said Janelle with a kind smile that seemed so out of place for the situation as she expertly pushed the knife just a little further up under his breast bone to get at that special pulsing piece of meat that gives life with its labors.

"Whaa…" Aaron could feel the darkness pulling at him, the light fading from his eyes. His body went limp and he felt himself being dragged. The air felt dry and the temperature dropped fast. Janelle had dragged him with seeming effortlessness into the cooler to die. A place as cold as her disturbing words had been earlier. How ironic he thought. "I left a man to die and here I am, getting left to die as well." These were his last thoughts as oblivion claimed him.

Janelle had moved him quickly onto a sheet of plastic there in the cooler where she had all the tools she needed within easy reach. Stripping his clothing and piercing his Achilles tendon just so, she pulled him up with her hand cranked winch. Humming while she slit his throat for some of the blood to drain and getting ready to gut him she worked contentedly thinking what a success her bar had become since she had taken over.

It seemed that she was blessed in what she did, almost as if fate itself brought her these fools who had narrowly escaped death allowing her to use them without having to worry about someone looking for them. This one would surely be thought lost in the forest where he came from after the car accident. As for the dogs that might follow the scent she would simply scrub the floor lovingly as she always did and throw in a little extra spice in the water and lay down a new coat of wax so that the chemical smell might confuse the animal. Either way this was a public place, and many people came and went for her special steaks and burgers with their beer.

Her biggest worry in the beginning when the first of these lost souls had tried to rob her had been how to dispose of the organs and bones. Janelle was a thorough woman however, and she simply cooked everything that was left until it was falling off the bones. In the last year she had gained a great deal of practice and once bones were properly boiled they became brittle and easily ground. The calcium they contained were part of what made her tomato garden the envy of all her neighbors. The organs, and skin, and flesh that she couldn't serve she would turn into a hearty stew for her beloved dogs. Each of which weighed nearly fifty pounds with their lean healthy bodies, each of them now so different from the scrawny mutts she had rescued from the pound.

In the beginning she had found the intestines the most difficult to deal with, mainly because she had to clean them before she could cook them for her beloved pets. This too she always found a way to deal with. It was a simple matter to follow the esophagus up far enough to cut in half and then tie off, and do the same with the other end of the intestines. So easily contained until she could get the majority of the mess out of the large and small intestines out into a bucket she kept handy for just this purpose.

Always as she worked she was brought back to that first time when she had killed her husband here in his bar. He had beaten her badly a month before and she was just getting over his last attack when she was working late trying to clean as quickly as she could so he wouldn't be angered. A patron had been in the bathroom still after they had locked the doors; it was when this patron intervened that they killed each other. Her husband from a stab wound to the heart, and the patron from a head injury that would take days to claim his life.

She remembered specifically the moment she stabbed her husband while the patron attempted to pull him off of her. She could almost feel once again the hot gush of his life's blood as it spilled out on her hands. Janelle could remember the sudden rage that exploded up from somewhere within her as she shoved the knife up into her husband's heart just that little bit further, and the grim satisfaction she felt when he could no longer take breath.

That was the first time Janelle had seen death up close and personal, it hadn't really bothered her to see her husband dead, or the stranger staggering around trying to maintain consciousness after hitting his head on a tables corner. When he had fallen she had wiped the handle of her knife with a bar towel and covered it once again with blood and placed it in the hand of the stranger who had given his life for her freedom. As the days passed she had been terrified that he would wake up and remember that she had been the one to take her husbands life. Afraid his stiff body would somehow rise from the dead, possessed by the demon inside him, with the soul purpose of making her pay.

She remembered the second time, more intimately, he had met death when a man had come into her bar to try to rob, and rape her. Her work at the bar lifting the heavy boxes of foodstuffs had made her stronger than she had ever been in her life. It was a simple matter to slip her sharp butcher knife up under his ribcage. Her aim had certainly gotten better she thought as she worked on her latest victim. Tomorrow she would have another one of her special stews that would bring people from all over the city. At first she had been confused by some of the new patrons who had shown up once she had made her first few specials from the bodies of dead fools. They were always women, and they were always rich, and they always made a point to subtly let her know that they knew the texture of her meat stew was unlike anything served anywhere else. At first these women had terrified her because she didn't want to be caught, and then one of them had given her a card with nothing but a number to a voicemail that requested a day, a location, and hours of operation. Now when Janelle called the number and left a message telling the day, and her hours of operation, and her special stew, women from all over the city, and sometimes from another state would arrive only to eat with carnivorous joy, and leave monstrous tips for all her waitresses.

With the patronage of these women Janelle had pulled her husband's failing bar up from the brink of bankruptcy into a thriving hotspot that had made her wonderfully rich in just a short time. Still there were more fools coming in from traumatic events without having called anyone. The ones who gave her the biggest thrill were the ones who thought she was easy prey. These were the bad men the world would never miss. These men always came with thoughts of rape and theft, and they met the real Janelle with the sure knowledge that the days when men were stronger than women were over.

She was happy now, her and her beloved dogs which she doted on every moment she was home. She was running the business so smoothly that there were never any unexpected problems. Janelle never had to worry about being short handed because her waitresses would fight over who got to work on stew days if she allowed it to happen. Her work in her bar, and in her garden at home kept her strong. She was vital, and still looked like a woman twenty years her junior. Such is the life, of Janelle. The woman who found her strength, and her place in the world by bringing death upon the unsuspecting, and the deserving, was also once the woman who had been beaten nearly to death by the first man she had murdered.

❖

Brothel

Friday Night
September 15th 1995
Lizard Lick Police Department, North Carolina
Case: Open

Incident Report:

Nicole Ray gets out of her car onto the wet asphalt from the recent rain storm and walks across the street to the big Victorian home in front of her. Nicole is a young woman. She is 5' 6" with a childish complexion. At 22, she looks more like a 17-year-old, but then again, where she is going it won't really matter. Nicole held her purse tight against her body. Afraid somebody might run by and take it from her? Perhaps. Maybe just a little paranoid of its contents being discovered.

As Nicole gets closer to the door she starts to think about what people might think if they saw her at that exact moment. She is wearing a pink snakeskin miniskirt two inches above mid-thigh. Her white slim-fit shirt pressed against her body accentuates her assets in a way only one type of women could manage. Slutty? No, she didn't think of herself as a slut. It was simply all part of the game. The minds of people could dance around the idea all day for all she cared. They would never understand her fully.

Nicole knocks on the door and waits as the clicks from heels gets closer. An old woman who presents herself as Lady Glendale opens the door and invites her in. She is dressed in an old fashioned dress you would expect a 1950's woman of status to wear, except Lady Glendale is a little on the heavyset side. Lady Glendale smiles at Nicole and leads the way through a richly ornate living room into a side hall. There they stop in front of a plain wooden door. Lady Glendale turns to Nicole and asks, "Is this your first time?" Nicole blushes a deep red and nods yes. "Don't worry about it too much hun. These guys are here for your pleasure. They have been naughty boys and need to be taught a lesson."

Nicole's confidence rises and she prepares to go down into the neon lit stairway leading to the basement. Lady Glendale grabs her arms and says, "Money first. There are no refunds if you decide to back out at the last minute."

With her newly found courage and determination, Nicole grins. "I don't think I will back out. Though it might be my first time I know I am mature enough to handle it."

"Whatever you say hun. It'll be two grand either way. Whether you go all the way or not."

"Is there any limits to what we can and cannot do with them?"

"Of course not, like I said, they are here for your pleasure. If you think you're up for it, do it. I have a couple of other girls down there right now. Some of them won't mind sharing if you want."

"It's okay. I am the jealous type. I want him all for myself."

"Suite yourself. I'm just running a business here." Lady Glendale holds out her hand in which Nicole lays 20 crisp $100 bills. Nicole walks down into the basement where she faces a hallway lined with doors ten deep on both sides. She walks down peering thru the small windows of the doors, getting a glimpse of what is going on inside. She can't help but feel aroused.

Nicole finally decides on a guy and opens the door. The man is sitting in a chair with his hands tied to it. She sets her purse near the door and walks to the man. Nicole sits on his lap rotates her body in a swirling movement in an effort to arouse him. When nothing happens down there, she stands up and slaps him. "Don't look at me like that. Am I not good enough for you? Is that what it is? Look at you. You look like a scared little dog. Pitiful."

She continues by raising her skirt up and taking of her shirt. She gives him an impromptu lap dance. She irritates after a minute and walks back to her purse. Nicole removes an item and walks back to the man. "Now, don't be too scared. This will only hurt for a minute."

With a few quick flicks of her hand, the man's eyeballs lay on the floor. It might be her first time paying for it, but certainly not the first time she has tortured a man to death. From the ceiling there is a hook on a chain. Though her 5' 6" stature might be unimpressive, she is strong. She raises the man up until his chin is slightly past the hook. She lets him fall. The man hanging from under his chin, body weight threatening to snap his neck, she begins to disembowel him.

After finishing she walks out and up the steps. Lady Glendale meets her and takes her to a washing room set up for the ladies when they are done with their business. The room is about 15x20 feet. Showers line the sides on every wall. Some girls are in there now recounting their experience with each other. Nicole showers, dresses and heads back out to her car. Though she likes the simplicity, she doesn't come back. We lose track of her after then.

J. Carlos Perez

Bury Your Dead

"Mom I think there's a monster under my bed."

"Mary-Anne what have I told you about bed monsters?"

"They're not real, they are a figment of my imagination....but I heard it."

"Go to sleep, there is nothing under your bed." *Nothing she'll ever know of,* the mother thought.

The mother went out to the living room where her date awaited.

"You look gorgeous Sally." The young man said.

Oh, but I know that, she thought. She scanned the floorboards, thinking where her latest victim would fit best. Perhaps next to her husband would be fine?

Carrie Looks The Other Way

Carrie opened the book, half watching over her shoulder, half peeping in. It'd taken her three days of snooping in her sister's room to find her diary and finally after so much work she was getting a chance to find out what her sister really thought of Jake, the current trend at school. Running her hand over the faux white leather, she felt goose bumps knowing she was seconds away from finding out what she'd been longing to know for so long.

Did she like him as well?

Though she was in her room, paranoia set in. What if her sister realized her diary was gone? Would she instantly be suspicious of her? Taking no chances she quickly opened the manicured journal and flipped through towards the latest entries.

"Life is shit. Why won't it just end?"

That wasn't like her sister at all. Why had she written that? Carrie flipped back and read more. Eyes open wide, she found entry after entry like the first she'd seen.

"Fuck my life."

She smiled a toothy grin. "At least Jake is mine for the taking."

J. Carlos Perez

Chapped Lips

Walking towards Christine's house, I instinctively reach into my pocket and pull out my ChapStick: Original strawberry flavor. The fact that I use ChapStick is girly enough so I stay away from extravagant flavors like winter-morning mint and honey blaze. I lightly coat my upper and lower lips with the soothing skin protectant. Damn winter months, they make my lips crack up like the Mohave Desert. I rub my lips together and then give them a quick flick of the tongue.

Maybe you're wondering why I would instinctively put on ChapStick while going to her house. I know I would be wondering the same. The thing is, every time I go to her house, she greets me with a kiss. Sure, we are not dating but that does not stop us. We have a mutual agreement to "friend rights."

I remember our first "friend" kiss as clear as the first time I saw a shooting star. It's an unforgettable moment that you witness for only one second, you point in awe and then it's gone. In a short instant the moment of perfection is gone. It was my first kiss of any kind.

It happened on our way back from an AFJROTC (Air Force Junior Reserve Officer Training Corps) field trip. Out of all places, we had gone to the bowling alley. I didn't know then and I still don't know now what the bowling alley had to do with what we were supposed to be learning in that class. I will not complain though, without the field trip, I would not have kissed her.

We played a game of bowling with some friends—Cesar, Robert, Casey. Then we went to the arcade section and raced each other on the two-player racing game. I was not very good at it and she beat me both times. I never really was that much into video games. After that we shot some pool, well at least we attempted to. I don't remember exactly during what round of the game she came over and hugged me but it was spontaneous, I do remember that. Also, I remember thinking, "Can this be so?"

The rest of the night we had stayed together pretty close. She was in my hands and I in hers. On the way back to school on the bus, I remember having an uneasy feeling in my stomach. Her fingers

174

were intertwined with mine in a perfect communion and her head rested softly on my shoulder. Now that I look back at things, I realize everything we talked about during that bus ride was irrelevant to anything we had talked about before. Our thoughts were a jumble of emotions, delirium of sorts.

You know when you are a little kid and you want to do something really bad but you're scared your mother will get onto you? You get that sick feeling in your stomach. Except it's a nervous feeling that makes you want to rip it out, well I was feeling it. I could feel my heart pumping loudly inside of my chest, begging to burst out of its confines. I wanted to just grab Christine's head and turn it towards mine. I wanted to lock eyes for a second, see into her very soul and then kiss her. Yet I could not bring myself to do it.

Eventually I did get her to turn around and kissed her. Though it all went very different than I had expected it to, overall it was good. I turned her around then realized I would not be able to lock into her eyes. It was pitch dark on the bus and I could barely see two millimeters in front of me. I went in for the kill and missed by a fraction of a foot. I felt embarrassed at first, but she helped in the confusion and got everything under control.

And boy did she take control of the situation. I felt like a little kid being guided by the hand by his mother into the playground for the first time. She dominated the entire experience but then again, I guess it made it that much more perfect. The only thing I managed to say after the kiss was, "mmm strawberry." The fruity taste of her lips bathed my senses in a way nothing else had ever done before. It was that same feeling I was going for every time I kissed her after that day.

Strawberry ChapStick on my lips. Ready to take on the world.

I walked up to her door and knocked. I could feel my lips craving for hers as she opened the door and I got a glimpse of her. Her hazel brown eyes pierced me like daggers; her luscious soft lips teased me. I moved in to kiss her but was fended off by a turn of the cheek. I did not understand. Just the other day everything had been great between us.

"I've recently discovered I like girls more than I do boys. I hope you can understand."

I thought, *what the fuck are you insane?* Then I just nodded my head and walked away. My three-month enchantment was now over.

The wind blew hard as I walked towards my house. Content without a doubt of remorse, I applied a thin coat of classic spearmint ChapStick.

❖

Cold Case

Her name was Denise Olsen. She was 19 with cobalt blue eyes, dirty blonde hair and studying medicine at Wake Forest University. She was driving to her parent's house for Thanksgiving dinner when she was killed by someone closer to her than anyone can imagine.

Her body was found lying on a boardwalk in front of a waterfall. None of her personal belongings were recovered from her body except a pack of Camel Menthols, which weren't even hers. Her cell phone was missing. The keys to her car were missing. Her car was missing. Though a prime suspect had been held in custody charged with Denise Olsen's murder, they were later released after their alibi held up. The case is still open but it's reached a standstill. The case has gone indefinitely cold.

On the morning of November 25th 2010, Denise had been in her dorm room until 11 A.M. at which time she got up and went into the dorms kitchen where her roommate had breakfast ready. Jessie Mack was 21 and a habitual smoker—Denise was not. They took turns cooking breakfast, alternating every other day. That morning Jessie had cooked egg, cheese and bacon omelets with a side dish of grapes and low-cal yogurt. Both the girls took care of their bodies to a level of extremes. They were perfect imitations of the other. Expect one smoked and the other didn't. That's why they made a good couple.

"When are you going to tell your parents babe?" asked Jess. She crossed her legs and sat Indian style in the chair.

"Soon."

"You've been saying that for over 5 months. I know your parents come from a religious background but I know they will accept you for what you are."

"And what's that? Lesbian?"

"No. A smart doctor to be. You being a lesbian has nothing to do with your character. Your parents will see that and accept it like my parents did with me."

"What if they don't? What if they hate me?" Denise was sitting now. Though she had been famished when entering the kitchen, the nervous nature of the conversation had ruined her appetite.

"They won't. I know it." Jess opened her carton of Camel Menthols and plucked out a cigarette, placing it in her mouth she lit up as Denise's countenance changed from worried to anger.

"You know I don't like it when you smoke in here."

"It's Thanksgiving, live a little. What time are you going to your parents place?"

"Probably late. Around 5 or 6. Do you want to come with?"

"I don't know. I am a little more open with my lesbianism. Are you sure you want your mom to know you are sharing a dorm with a lesbian. Much less let her know that roommate is your girlfriend?"

"Know what? I want you to be there. I don't want to keep hiding you away. I am not embarrassed by you and I want the whole world to know I love you."

"Are you sure? I wasn't trying to pressure you into telling them today. I mean."

"I want to do it. I'll tell my mother by phone and hopefully she will tell me father for me. I just can't deal with telling him."

"I love you."

"I love you too, more than you know."

Jess finished her breakfast and went to the bathroom to take a shower Meanwhile Denise paced the living room building up courage to call home.

It had been a sunny morning that day. A record high for that time of year. It felt like there wouldn't be a winter. Many hoped that was true considering the year before had brought heavy snow fall throughout the triad counties.

As the phone rang, Denise could feel her heart beginning to thump harder inside her chest. Thump, thump, thump, faster and faster it thumped. When the phone was picked up on the other line it stopped. She was frozen silent.

"Hello?" It was her younger brother, Matt. "Hello? Who is this? Is anyone there? I am going to hang up if you don't talk."

Denise swallowed hard and said, "Matt, it's me Denise. Can you put mom on the phone please?"

"Denise, why the hell do you have to be such a creeper? I thought you were prank calling."

"Matt just put mom on."

"Okay geez."

Denise heard her brother Matt call out for his mom and immediately her heart started to speed up again. "Hello? Denise is something wrong?"

"Uhh hey mom. No, nothing is wrong. I just wanted to ask you something."

"Okay."

"Can I bring someone to Thanksgiving dinner tonight?"

"Well, it's something special I usually try to keep within family. You know how it is."

"Mom this person is very special to me. I would really love it if you met her."

"Her?"

"Yes mother. Her name is Jessie Mack. She's my roommate at the University and she and I are dating." Her heart stopped beating and time seemed to come to a stop. She could hear her mother breathing on the line but neither was saying anything. She wanted to give her some time to digest things. Sure enough her mother piped up after a few minutes.

"Well in that case, sure bring her along. I want to meet her first though. How about we meet up at Lou's before you two come here?"

"Uhh that sounds fine with me. I'll let Jess know. Mom I love you."

"I love you too Denise. Be careful."

"I will mom. Bye." Denise but the phone down with a weight lifted from her chest. Her secret was out.

Jess walked out of the bathroom wrapped in a white towel. She stopped at the doorway leading into the living room. "How did it go?" she asked. "Did your mother flip out?"

179

"No. Actually I think she took it fairly well. She wants to meet you thought, before dinner tonight."

"I'm sure that is going to be fun, having her scrutinize me to determine if I am worthy enough for you or better yet, her standards."

"She said to meet up with her a Lou's at 4."

"I will meet you there. I have a little errand to run first."

"Do you want me to go with you?"

"No. I need to do this alone. Besides it's a surprise."

"Oh yeah? And what kind of surprise could that be?"

"Don't worry your mind about that you hear. You have a report to write for O'Shay's class. What was it? Adverse effects caused by Vicotin on the human body?"

"Yeah, you are right. I'll be better prepared if I do a little work on it instead of procrastinating till the last minute. Anyways I already know I am going to love whatever your surprise may be."

"That's the spirit. Have fun with that paper."

Jess walked into the clinics lobby, smiled as the secretary acknowledged her presence and sat down in the same leather sofa as the day before. She laid her back against the cushion and stared off into the ceiling before closing her eyes. She let out a sigh and reminded herself why she was doing it. "To strengthen her relationship and protect her body," that's what she told herself as she waited.

"Jessie Marie Mack," the receptionist piped up startling Jess from her daydream.

"Dr. Novak will see you now."

"Thank you Alice." Jess walked past Alice into the doctor's office she had been lead to the previous visit. That's when everything had been explained to her. When she had willed herself into using her body as a guinea pig. "It's to strengthen my relationship," she repeated before walking into the doctor's office. That was day one of her clinical studies with a new pill that promised to eliminate her addiction to nicotine.

Denise brought her car to a stop in front of the metallic structure everyone knew as Lou's Dinner. It was a quaint restaurant owned by friends of the family. Generation through generation it had been passed down each time growing larger in popularity. People considered it a landmark and with all the tourists that came by each year to try the unique food Lou's offered, it most certainly had the reputation to be.

Denise looked at her phone to see if she had any new messages or missed calls from Jess; nothing. She found it strange Jess hadn't called ahead of time telling her she might be late to meet with her mother and herself. Denise sat in her car waiting until she saw her mother beckoning her by the boardwalk leading to a waterfall behind the restaurant. Though closed on most days, the Olsen family had always been in a tight niche with the Grisons, allowing them access anytime.

After locking her car, Denise followed the silhouette which was once her mother into the darkness. Towards the end of the boardwalk, near the waterfall, a single light post illuminated the surrounding darkness. Her mother was standing by the railing facing the waterfall. Denise walked up behind and said, "Hey mom. Jess will be here in a minute. She is running a little late."

"You mean you don't do everything together? You don't spend every minute of your day with her? How could you do this to our family?" her mother asked irately.

"I take it you don't approve of it."

"Approve of it? I would never approve of such blasphemy. You are going to hell and you know it."

"Mom you are hurting me. Why are you saying this to me?"

"You deserve it and more." Denise reached forward in an attempt to grab her mother to pull her in for an embrace. "Don't you dare touch me! I just wanted to let you know you and your friend are not welcome in my house. I don't care if I never see you again as a matter of fact."

"Mom," Denise reached forward again crying. This time her mother pushed her away with brute force. Denise stumbled backward, tripping on her feet before hitting the back of her head against the sharp corner of the wooden railing. Her body fell to the floor limp.

Mrs. Olsen stood back agape. Her daughter wasn't moving. She wasn't breathing. Mrs. Olsen had killed her daughter by accident. "What will they think of me?" she thought. "I can't go to jail." Mrs. Olsen reached into her purse and removed a cigarette—Camel Menthol. The time passed as Mrs. Olsen paced around her daughter's body trying to figure out what to do. Cigarette after cigarette she smoked until the perfect idea came to mind. "If somebody has to pay it's her girlfriend" she thought. "It's her fault we even had this discussion. If she hadn't turned my daughter into a monster, I wouldn't have done this."

Mrs. Olsen removed all of Denise's personal items and left her on the floor surrounded by cigarette butts and the empty box she had smoked through. She drove away in Denise's car to God knows where. It was never recovered. An hour later a cab dropped her off at Lou's. She was back at the crime scene ready to play her part as a distressed mother. She called the police and reported the death of her daughter.

When questioned she said she had been late to a planned meeting between her daughter and her friend. Mrs. Olsen denied being a smoker and suggested they investigate Denise's roommate at Wake Forest University. The fact Jess and Mrs. Olsen smoked the same cigarettes had been a coincidence Mrs. Olsen hadn't expected. The evidence pointed Jess's way. The only thing lacking was motive.

Jess was picked up on I-77 just outside of King. She claimed to have been at Hanes Mall shopping for something to give Denise, an alibi that checked out the next day when the officers were able to question workers at Victoria Secret that had assisted Jess during her shopping.

Her name was Denise Olsen. She was 19 with cobalt blue eyes, dirty blonde hair and studying medicine at Wake Forest University. She was driving to her parent's house for Thanksgiving dinner when she was killed.

J. Carlos Perez

David

A sharp sudden knock on the door jolts Ian from his trance like state. He rubs his eyes and looks at his mother lying in the bed next to him, chest heaving with each hard laborious breath. The room is cold yet her forehead is beaded in sweat. Her face is pale and clammy. Her eyes mere slits, unable to open completely due to exhaustion. Ian grips his mother hand and says, "Don't worry mother. He has come. He will help take you away from your misery. Don't fear." Another knock and Ian walks to the front door.

Ian opens the door and looks at the man. He is younger than Ian expected, better looking too. The man dressed in a black suit extends his arm and presents himself as David. Ian welcomes the man and apologizes for the house being so cold. "I've been inside taking care of my mother all day. Didn't have time to get firewood," he explains. "It's quite alright. I find working at this temperature better anyways," David says cunningly. "Of course, however you please sir." Ian feels compelled to stare at the man. His calm face and low shoulders. Ian swore he'd seen him before, at Aunt Belinda's funeral perhaps? "Where is she? I would like to get this over with as soon as possible" David says. "Of course, follow me this way." Ian leads the man through the living room into a hall lined with two doors on each side. "One leads to the basement, one to the kitchen, one to a bathroom and the other to my mothers room," Ian explains. Why he explains everything to the stranger he doesn't know. Out of courtesy perhaps?

Ian opens the door and walks to his mother side. "Mother, David is here. He is going to help you." His mother struggles to open her eyes but fails; it's all too much for her. David steps over the other side of the bad and extends his hand. "Loretta come with me. Walk with me for a while," he says. "You promise I won't feel anything?" she struggles to say. "Yes I promise your pain will go away. Everything will go away. It will be better."

Loretta takes David's hand and raised herself up. The floor felt warm beneath her bare feet. Effortlessly she and David walked out of the room, leaving Ian next to a cold lifeless body. He didn't remember when his father had died but he knew he was feeling the same thing his mother had felt then. Great sadness yet relieved knowing she moved on to a better place. He wondered, "Who's going to watch me die?"

J. Carlos Perez

Death at a Party

I sit in my car watching rain drops pelt the windshield, trying their hardest to force themselves in. Outside a white wall of rain blankets the way to the office doors where my boss is standing with towels, handing them to employees as they eagerly approach the warmth of the building. I've been watching his fake smiles from across the parking lot and I can't help but feel sick. This man is pretending so hard to be liked, yet when he gets home he'll curse the names of every employee. Denouncing their stupidity and how bad they are "fucking up" his company image.

Today is no ordinary day. Today is his birthday. Avery Wittington didn't make it mandatory for workers to attend his after work party at the office, but he'll keep a mental note of everyone who didn't come. When it's time to give employees a pay raise he will remember who didn't show up for his birthday and find an excuse to exclude them.

I know this well because Avery Wittington is my father.

The rain outside continues to pour and has now been joined by loud thunder. The blue arches of death flash across the sky, brightening the day for a second later to leave it a dark paradise again.

I wonder to myself how grand it would be if I walked out and on my way to the devil, lightning struck me dead before his eyes. Death at a party, how grand.

Engulfed in my own fantasy, I step outside and strut towards the office doors. As I walk I repeat to myself, "Strike me God. Fucking do it you pussy!" Of course, if there is a God, he wouldn't strike me just in spite. No, he'd make me live my life in this hell on earth.

I walk up to the double-faced man and say, "Happy fucking birthday." I smile a fake smile and take the towel he's handing me. One day, I'll be like my father.

❖

Evil Alien Scum

With his backpack in his hands, eyes locked on the floor, Zachary walked up his driveway to where his mother was watching him get off the bus. She could tell from afar something was wrong. The way Zach was walking in a ditzy manner, sort of like a drunk and the fact he was walking so slowly towards her. He usually ran off the bus, bouncing around like a tempest.

Zach was in the first grade with an overactive imagination and still very timid of the big school environment. He was afraid of the teachers the most. He saw them as ugly Martian monsters. Though he did not know what they were exactly, he had seen enough of them on TV to know they could not be good. He was afraid that at any second they were going to pull out a laser gun and blast him into a pile of ashes, especially if he did something wrong.

After a few days of school, he had learned a good way to trick those lousy scumbags. All he had to do was do what they said and he got a smile and a sucker—he still doubted whether or not the sucker was poisoned. During the first week of class, he learned three important things that made Mrs. Ears mad the most (pronounced like airs, weird I know but what can you do).

First, she hated tattletales. The worst thing you could do was tell on somebody else. Trevor McGregor had made the mistake of tattling on the second day and he had paid the consequences dearly. Right before recess, Mrs. Ears walked to the closet behind her desk and pulled out the tattletale. It was a long white rope with a resizable loop. If you were a tattletale, you might as well wear your tale, she had said.

Second was tidiness. Everything had its proper place inside of the desk. Every paper was to be properly organized in its color-coded folder and every pencil in its designated pouch, color pencils in one and regular pencils in another—strictly forbidden of course, the mechanical pencil. Nobody had gotten in trouble for having an unorganized desk yet and Zach feared the consequence for that offense. Maybe she'll make you carry your stuff with you everywhere, he thought.

However, the greatest and ill of offenses was one that Zach

paid the most attention to. DO NOT WRITE IN YOUR BOOK. Mrs. Ears said it repeatedly until it lay embedded into his mind. He slept thinking about not writing in the book. Mind control is how she done it, at least that's what Zach thought. Whenever he had a book out on his desk, he made sure his pencil was nowhere near it. If possible, he kept it in his desk while the book was out. If telling on somebody resulting in embarrassment, and untidiness resulted in— well he didn't know but he knew it had to be bad, then the act of writing in school property must get him a hundred years in prison. Worse, maybe she would take him to her leaders and have them probe him. That very thought made him shiver.

And today, he had done the unthinkable. On his way home from school on the bouncy, boring, dizzying bus he soiled his book. The smell of a fifth grader cucumber melon cream, the passing of a dead skunk and to make it worse, the smell of a cow field, all mixed together and punched his stomach with a ninjas fury. The small dizzy spell he got was nothing compared to the sensation before his dam broke. He could feel the vomit coming up to his mouth and caught it once. He swallowed it back down but was hit again with another wave soon after. There went lunch.

Not many of the other kids had said much to him about it. There wasn't to many kids left on the bus to get on to him though. The one thing that they all seemed to care about was the smell. Apparently his vomit was smellier that then smell of the skunk, cow manure and surprisingly enough, the cucumber melon lotion. Zach didn't see what the big deal was about the smell. He wanted to scream at them, "Get over it, it's just a smell. Look what I did to the book." However, when he tried talking, he could feel his stomach turning over another beat. Instead, he just waited until he got home and walked off the bus with his backpack in his hands, eyes locked on the floor.

Halfway up his driveway, his mother starting walking towards him, obviously cluing into the fact something was wrong with him. His eyes started to water and followed milliseconds behind by the burst of another damn, this time the one behind the eyes. Streams of tears flowed from his eyes and ran down his face.

"Honey what's wrong?"

"Mommy, the Martian teacher is going to kill me."

"What? Why? What did you do hun?"

"I threw up on the book."

"Is that all? She is not going to kill you for that silly, there is no harm done. We will simply buy the book from the school and they will get a new one."

"You sure?"

"Of course I am sure; I did the same thing when I was your age."

"That doesn't count. Your teachers weren't evil alien scum."

J. Carlos Perez

Finding My Feet

On Wednesday, January 29th Roger Holland woke up as he usually did. He let the alarm clock ring exactly three times before hitting the snooze button. He looked at his watch lying next to the alarm clock and checked their accuracy down to the last second. Roger got up from his bed, left foot first off the right side, and walked the 27 steps to the bathroom, counting each step as he went along. He looked at himself in front of the mirror to check for any abnormal changes then proceeded to undress himself. Left sock first, then the right one, followed by his pajama bottoms, shirt, and finally boxers. Roger showered for 10 minutes exactly.

Roger Holland left his apartment at exactly 7:49 with 30 seconds and headed for 5th and Grand where he would wait for the bus for five minutes. At 8 he would make himself comfortable as best he could in the odd numbered seat on the back of the bus. Roger talked to no one as he waited, he never did. Strangers asked him the time as 8 o'clock passed but Roger didn't respond. Roger Holland kept his gaze down counting as he tapped his feet in intervals of two, corresponding with the seconds. 60 seconds, 120 taps. At 8:10 the bus finally came and Roger made his way back to his regular empty seat. A girl he'd been standing next to at the bus stop followed him to the back and sat down next to him. He noted the polka dotted dress she was wearing: three purple dots followed by a red square, repeating all over. He knew she was going to talk to him. He could feel it. He counted the seconds as they went by ...59, 60, 61, 62... "What were you doing?" she asked finally. He waited 3 seconds then responded "What was I doing when?" The girl with four pimples, three bracelets on her left hand, two rings on her right responded "Right now. At the bus stop. You were counting to yourself while staring down. Mighty suspicious if you ask me." Three more seconds and Roger responded, "I was watching my feet. Didn't want to lose count of time."

190

Fragments (Wee Challenge 44)

*a Wee Challenge is a challenge to tell a complete story in less than a certain amount of words.

I remember Dobson, one year ago. Completely out of breath from the sight of her, I asked for her name. I shouldn't have done that. I sit and stir the fragments of my splintered heart, spilled on the floor. She left a month ago. The revolver laying on the desk, waiting for one final shot. To end her life.

J. Carlos Perez

His New Friend

Little Matthew was 5 years old and loved going outside, exploring the garden behind his house that to his perspective appeared enormous. It was there that he found it. He had never seen one before and maybe that's why it caught his attention as it chewed on his mother's roses. It looked so pure...so mystical...so green. To you and me it would have looked like a regular old green caterpillar and the truth is, it was. But too little Matthew it was something, new some kind of a mystery.

Soon enough he had ran back to his house, found a glass jar, and had put the caterpillar in the jar with some leaves and a rose for it to chew on. It was then that his mother, wondering what he was doing decided to go check on him. She found him lying on the ground staring at the glass jar as if expecting something mystical to happen at any moment. She picked up the jar, not knowing that there was a caterpillar in it and was going to throw it away when little Matthew cried out in a relentless effort to save his newly acquired friend. And of course his mother wondering why he was crying looked down at the jar and saw it. The green caterpillar that was on one of the leaves as if nothing was happening around it. She explained to him that she needed to put a lid on the jar and poke holes in the lid so the caterpillar could breath and so that it couldn't get out. Little Matthew didn't care what she did to the jar of course all he wanted was to be able to keep his new friend.

For weeks after that little Matthew would spend hours on end staring...watching...hoping that his caterpillar would do something impressive, but it didn't. It simply chewed on the leaves and got bigger and fatter. Little Matthew was not amused no more and went looking for other things that might do something. That same day his father came home with a new pet for his son...a little puppy. This of course thrilled little Matthew and made him forget entirely of the caterpillar for days. Until one day he heard a loud crash in his room and wondered what it was.

As he stepped in the room he immediately knew what had happened. His puppy had run into the table in his room knocking over the glass jar. He looked everywhere but could not find the

192

caterpillar…he wondered if his puppy had ate it. Little Matthew looked behind his dresser…under his bed…it was nowhere. The only thing different in his room was a flying little critter that kept bothering him as he tried to find his old friend.

J. Carlos Perez

Januaries First Snow

It was a mid-winter day and the wind was blowing particularly hard. The temperature was 24 degrees Fahrenheit but the wind chill factor was well below zero. It had not snowed yet and it was unlikely there would be a first snow of the winter that year. For the past few years, it had snowed less and less in Dobson. Even though everybody knew why it had been snowing less and less with each passing year, nobody wanted to straight up point their finger at global warming caused big city pollution.

Surry Central had the same atmosphere around it that it always attracted after the Christmas holiday. The teachers, having had a break from the troublesome students were now refreshed and ready to give their days worth. The students not so happy about being back, yet still willing to go for their own sake.

At 7:25 in the cold Wednesday morning, the heart of the school was giving its first few good beats. With those few hard thumps warming the vast interior to those who arrived early. The buses would start arriving around 7:30 and with the arrival of the buses, the school would spin into full gear. Dozens of students would swarm the cafeteria for a warm biscuit and hot cappuccino, stuffing their mouths with second-rate food and warming their bodies with the hot foamy liquid.

Grayson Paton Piers (goes by Paton) was leaning nonchalantly against a pair of thin-brown hot pipes that ran from the radiator to the vent on the roof. On cold winter mornings, those pipes were the most loved objects in the eyes of Paton. The heat radiating off them was hot to the touch; but when wearing a hoodie, they provided a warm feeling on the back that warmed him.

Looking out past the frost glazed panes of glass, Paton could see a bright red Cardinal sitting on a tree branch. The Cardinal was not eating, it was not chirping; it was simply sitting on the branch looking beautiful like God had planned it to look. In his mind Paton imagined the ground covered with a layer of thick white snow, the tree branches lightly sprinkled and the Cardinal standing out clearly in all its glory; the red of its feathers sharply making a contrast to the white precipitation on the ground.

194

Captivated by the Cardinal, Paton did not see his friend slowly creep up once seeing Paton was lost in thought. Vester Waldo jumped in from of Paton, grabbed him by the shoulders, and shook him half to death. "Paton man, vhat in the world is you doing? Expecting that bird to lay a golden egg or somethin?" Vester was a foreign exchange student from Germany and talked English with a heavy German accent. Sometimes it was impossible to understand what he was saying but it added something to the conversation.

Paton snapped back into reality with a thud, banging his head against the hot pipes behind him. "No, no. I was just....I was just uh thinking." Not the smartest way to lie out of the particular situation but it wasn't like Vester was going to believe him anyways, Paton thought.

"Oh yea, u vere thinken about das Mädchen from physics class." As he said this, Vester flashes his hugest toothy smile.

"What? I do not understand German. How many times am I going to have to tell you?" Paton was not bothered with Vester talking German; in fact, he enjoyed it when Vester talked German. It gave him a chance to learn something and making Vester repeat himself was priceless. Vester always got a "what are you stupid?" kind of look on his face that made Paton chuckle.

"I said the girl in class, you thinken about hur."

"Umm sure Vester lets go with that." Even though Paton had not been thinking about her at that particular moment, the mere mention of her get his mind whirling in a shrew of emotions.

Kendra Bryn was a slim, middle-height, junior in his Physics class. She had it all; she was blonde, had blue-green eyes, an IQ that easily out matched anybody who dared challenge her, everything. During the first day of class, they were allowed to chose their seat wherever they wanted. Not many teachers ever allowed that and Paton took full advantage of it. Even though he did not sit with Kendra, she ended up next to him either way. Paton had taken a seat on the third row from the back. It was a feeling of equality that he hungered that had ultimately won his decision of where to sit. Being right in the middle of the class gave him the best of both worlds. He was close enough to the front to hear every word the teacher said and he was far enough to where he could take an occasional nap. Little did he know when he chose that seat, Kendra Bryn also had a knack for being in the middle. Needless to say, Paton had not taken a nap in class once.

They talked often, in and out of class. He spent more time with her than he would have ever imagined. They were like two peas in a pod. They would always be together every chance they got. If you were to ask anybody from school, they would swear that they were going out. Yet, they were not. Paton was shy about expressing his feelings for her. He kept a notebook in which he would write love poems about her but never showed them to her. Paton had tried doing it once but decided she would think he was a loser for writing poetry. Instead of asking her out, he just went on contemplating whether she would say yes if he did ask her out.

The morning bell rung, earsplitting clang that always made Paton's ears hurt. He said goodbye to Vester and then went on the Physics, his favorite class of the day. Paton walked into physics class a few seconds before the tardy bell rang. He did it every day. His teacher, Sherrie McPherson, hated when students were not in their seats with the material for the day out and ready to go when the bell rang.

As he walked to his seat, he gave a couple of high fives to some of his friends along the way and then took his seat next to Kendra. He had not noticed it on his way in but Kendra was dressed up a little more than usual. She was always a sharp dresser, nothing formal but nothing shabby like ripped jeans. Kendra's hair was up in a way that Paton did not know if it had a special name but if it did, it was surely some weird French name.

Paton took out his physics book and binder and then continued to ignore Mrs. McPherson. "Hey, why are you so dressed up today? Is something special going on today? It's not picture day is it?"

"Oh this, it's nothing. And picture day was two weeks ago." Her tone was neither sad nor angry; it was a mix of the two. Paton had not realized it, but he had hurt her feelings by not remembering her birthday. Kendra raised her hand and without waiting for recognition from Mrs. McPherson, she blurted out, "I think I'm feeling sick. Can I call home?"

"I should make you stay after for interrupting my class, but since you say you're sick I will let you off this one time."

Taking no time to pack her stuff up, Kendra walked out with her books in her hands. Paton sat in dismay as Kendra left the room. She was not sick, he knew she was not sick. "I must have said something to piss her off", Paton thought. He tried to pay attention for the remainder of class but in the back of his head, the last conversation he had had with Kendra was playing repeatedly. He just could not find anything wrong in what he had said. It must be something else, maybe she is feeling sick, Paton thought.

After physics class Paton had AP American History, Honors E-Commerce, and then finally Trigonometry. During American History, he had a test in which he struggled to finish. Paton's head was not entirely focused in the exam. E-Commerce went by without a glitch. Creating websites was something Paton was good at doing and Mrs. York did not care what the students did in class. As long as they got their work done, she let them be. Trigonometry was the toughest of his classes and he hated it. The only reason he was taking it was that it was required for the college degree he was hoping to get into. Mrs. Chilton was a witch of a woman, taking nothing less than perfect as an answer. He still remembered his first day in her class. The night before he had went to sleep late watching a marathon of How Its Made on the Discovery Channel and was falling asleep during class. Mrs. Chilton had chewed him out saying that if he thought she was boring to leave the class because it was only going to get worse. Needless to say, math class passed slower than it had since the first day.

The afternoon bell rang to a welcome glee from all the students. If you were to measure the aura of relief around the students, you would get a high dose around Paton. On his way to the lobby, he took a few minutes to stand under a Dogwood tree and talk to his friends. He made plans to go to the Coffee Bean and then headed on up to the lobby. He usually waited up front with Kendra until her mom picked her up, but since she had left he did not really know what he would do. He could drive on home, the last place he wanted to be after school, or he could just hang out in the lobby until sometime passed. He settled on the latter.

Paton dropped his backpack on the concession stand. It was hardly ever open and everybody used it to put their duffel bags, book bags, and sit on it. He sat there for a moment, leaning his head against the side of the concession stand thinking about Kendra. When he saw Jessica Hanes walking towards the lobby, he waved at her and motioned her to go over to where he was. Jessica Hanes was a slim athletic girl. She played women's soccer, volleyball, and basketball. She had straight brown hair to her shoulders. Her face had razor sharp features, her eyes a piecing emerald blue, her face was free of blemishes and she was proud of that fact. Paton had dated her when they were in middle school, before she had matured into the beauty she was now, but it had not worked out between them long. Even though many say you can't stay friends with your ex's, their friendship had not suffered at all. They were young kids back then. They were not really in love, they just liked being together.

"Hey, how you doing?" Paton got down from the stand and hugged Jessica. There was something about hugs that brought tranquility to him, even if for a second.

"I'm good, but these tests are killing me."

"I know what you mean. Fowler is about to burst my kidney with his history tests."

"Yeah, so I can't believe you forgot."

"Forgot about what? Was I supposed to call you or something yesterday?"

"No, about today being Kendra's birthday."

"Her birthday is not today, I would have remembered."

"Well apparently your memory is smaller than a goldfishes. I saw her this morning in the lobby; she said she was waiting for her mom to pick her up. I said happy birthday to her and she started crying. I wondered for a minute why she would cry, I figured it was because she thought it a nice thing to do or something. But then I asked her and she said that you forgot. It really hurt her you know."

"But today is not her birthday. Her birthday is not until the 13th."

"No, that's her sister's birthday, hers is today."

"No wonder..." Paton was talking more to himself than to

Jessica but the words were still coming out of his mouth.

After a few minutes of awkward silence, Jessica chirped in drastically changing what they were talking about with an irrelevant remark. "So did you hear that it's supposed to snow sometime soon?"

"Jessica I uh got to go. I need to do something very important."

As he got his stuff and headed out the doors, Jessica screamed at him. "You better not make her cry anymore."

On his way over to his house, Paton kept thinking how he was going to pull a miracle off and get Kendra to forgive him. He thought about just apologizing and saying he was sorry for forgetting but that wouldn't work. He needed to do something special for her, something she had never had done, something that would flatter her off of her feet and into his arms, something that would stun her and melt her emotions.

Paton pulled into his driveway, said a quick "I'm home" to his mom once inside, and headed to his room just as fast. He threw his stuff on his desk and then did what he did best; he wrote. Words had never been quicker in spilling from his pen onto the paper. They flowed like an overflowed river on a steep incline. With every inch forward, it sped up as gravity pulled it by the reigns. As he wrote he hummed along with the lines. Laying a music infused bed of cotton for the words to lay upon.

When he was done writing, he opened his closet and took out his guitar. It had once belonged to his grandfather, an expert at playing it, but when he died he passed it on to Paton. Paton took it upon himself to try to be just as good as his grandfather had been with the guitar. He practiced every day and night for a few months after his grandfather's death but never thought he was getting as good as him. Pretty soon he came down to just occasionally playing it when he felt down. He played just as well as his grandfather but he would never admit to it. Again he hummed his beat in his head as his fingers glided over the frets, encompassing the room in a melodic harmony many could only dream of doing.

With his heart thumping louder than ever, he took his guitar and went to his car. He felt his stomach coming up to his throat, nervousness crawling up through his spine and immobilizing him and blurring his vision. Paton drove to Kendra's house and parked in the driveway. Just like in a romantic fairy tale story, Paton picked up small pebbles and threw one by one at her window. He might have stopped throwing them for fear of breaking the window, but fear was not able to surface. Nervousness was dominating the battlefield of his emotions.

Kendra opened her window, sticking her head out enough to be seen clearly, and said. "What do you want?"

"I just wanted to uhh tell you something."

"Well spill it. It's cold outside and the air is coming in."

"Listen I am sorry that I forgot your birthday, I would have never dreamed of doing it. I know that it hurt you and I really want you to know how sorry I am."

"Sometimes sorry just doesn't cut it."

"I know, I know, that's why I came here with my guitar. I wrote a song for you that I want you to hear."

Paton reached into the car and pulled out his guitar. Without saying another word to Kendra, he started strumming the guitar. With eyes wide shut he sang. The last words in his song where the words he had been wanting to ask since the first day he had meet her. "Will you go out with me?"

Unaware to Paton, Kendra shut the window and went to the front door. She missed a part of the song but it still held its meaning. The song hit hard at heart and brought more tears to her eyes. Nobody had ever written a song about her much less sung it to her before. He had given her the best present she could have asked for, though it was a bit late. As Paton opened his eyes, Kendra wrapped her arms around his neck, whispered "yes" into his ear, and kissed him as the first flakes of snow started to fall from the sky. Januaries first snow, melting around the radiance of their love.

❖

The Little Things

The flash is what I will remember the most. It was unlike anything I'd ever seen before. It was unworldly; ethereal. Everything after that flash will simply remain a scarred memory I choose to forget.

I'd been taking pictures that day: an assignment for a digital photography course I was taking. Up in the Blue Ridge Parkway, the natural beauty of North Carolina was surreal. Everything from the animals to the flowers had enticed me to keep shooting throughout the day. Though I had spent almost all day taking pictures of animals, what I'd really been looking forward to that day was a landscape shot from the scenic outlook during sundown.

I'd spent most of the day hiking trough trails and capturing what I thought to be the better things with the world. That is my vision. I didn't want to take pictures of things that were wrong with the world. I didn't want to raise awareness about pollution or other ecological problems. My vision is to celebrate everything that is right with the world.

After going through one 8GB memory card I'd settled down by my Jeep and passed most of the early afternoon playing solitaire. Right before sunset—which every real photographer will tell you is the magic hour—I drove down to the scenic outlook and set up my equipment. The birds were chirping just right, the autumn colors were perfect, everything was ideal for a great picture. What I hadn't been expecting was the explosion.

Usually when taking pictures of objects that are moving, I'll put the camera in continuous drive mode so that it keeps taking a picture every 1/3rd of a second and that day hadn't been different. There were a couple of eagles flying in the sky that caught my attention because of how they seemed to glow from the sun's rays. I'd been about to turn off the camera to change the lens when it happened. First there had been a bright flash towards Pilot Mountain and then came a sound that of like thunder. As soon as I'd seen the flash I'd hit the lock button on my remote and jumped inside of my Jeep. The pictures I took aren't important to me though. If I wasn't a photographer by nature, I would burn the pictures.

You would think an event like a nuclear attack on the US would send the country into chaos, but luckily, our leaders had plans. Ever since President Truman, the country has had a specific order of procedure in case of nuclear war or other such catastrophic event. This procedure is called COG (continuity of government). Though the attack on the US did include a bombing of Washington DC, killing the current President, Vice-president and most of the congressman, there were already other leaders ready to act. That was part of the plan. We don't know who these guys are or where they are hidden. We just know they are well secured along the eastern coast. I don't worry for the well being of the government. The United States is a strong nation and it will see it through. But that day all I cared about was my family. That was another marvel. Even with the world turned upside down, I managed to locate my family. My mother had already been in the hospital even before the attacks. She was pregnant. My father, well, they located him for me.

I was sitting in my mother's hospital room with my brother cuddled in my arms. His body moving up and down with each breath he took. My mother was in bed sleeping, weary from recent childbirth.

With my brother in my arms, I hadn't been able to resist contemplating the fact that I would never be able to hold my own son in my arms. I would never be able to have a son period. I will never get to pass on the gift of life because I have congenital adrenal hyperplasia. The decease made me hit puberty at an early age, causing many changes in my body normal men don't go through. One of those changes made me sterile. Even though my newborn brother is only that, my brother, he feels like a son to me. He is the closest I am going to get to have a baby in my arms, who is a small part of me—even if it is brotherhood.

I had my brother wrapped in a blue bunny blanket: it used to be mine. I'd had the blanket stored away hoping one day I would be able to give my son the same blanket I had slept many warms nights in. I'd thought I would never be able to pass it on to somebody after I heard of my condition but after many years my mother had come through. For eighteen years my mother had wanted another boy. We'd all given up hope when she reached her mid-thirties but at the last possible minute, she surprised my two sisters and me. At the age of forty my mother had another son and I finally got to pass on my blanket.

I'd put his hand in mine and was marveled by the clearer picture of exactly how small he was. His hand was the size of my pinky and his whole arms was the size of my hand—palm to fingertips. I'd sat in that room for hours. With the world thrown into chaos I didn't want to be thrown in with it. I wanted to enjoy the small things in life. Whatever life was left. The potential radiating from him was amazing. I'd thought of the future and the type of force that would be needed to somehow fix what had been broken for so long. Even before the bombs exploded so many things were wrong with the world. How could peace be achieved when the only thing governments were doing was shutting up the other by killing them. Was that peace? Maybe one day my brother will learn from the distraught earth and be the driving force required to fix it back to what our forefathers had imagined it to be.

My mother had then begun to wake from her slumber and I'd tried not to make noise in case she went back to sleep but my brother, sensing his mother was awake, began to whimper. I'd told my mom I'd take him outside for a bit so she could sleep some more but she was reluctant. "He's probably hungry," she'd said. I carried him to my mother's arms and told her I'd be back after she was finished feeding him. I exited the room half reluctantly knowing I still had other places I had to go.

Although it was two in the morning, the hospital halls were as busy as they had been in the afternoon. Normally I wouldn't have been allowed to visit my mother that late but she had no one else: my

father was in another hospital room two stories up. The nuclear
explosions had left all the local hospitals over-capacity, understaffed,
and running out of supplies. Our area hadn't been the only one to
suffer from an explosion but it was one of the worst after DC. It was
estimated there were more injured survivors than there were
unscathed people. But then again, that was to be expected.

My father had been working when the bombs made contact
with the ground. Even though the building he worked in was a mile
and a half from the epicenter of the explosion, the building wasn't
prepared for the force exerted. Nobody had been prepared for it.
Who would have thought terrorists would target a low populated area
in North Carolina?

My father hadn't seen his son yet and was doubtful he will.
He suffered a broken back, broken neck, massive blunt force trauma
to the head with implications of serious brain damage. The
neurosurgeons said that if my father survived he "may have profound
deficits."

I hadn't had the best of relations with my dad at the time but
with what was going on, everything that had driven me from him
seemed little. All I cared about was his health and well being. As I
walked towards the elevator I couldn't help but look at the carnage
around me. I was in the area which had been sectioned off for
pregnant mothers and less critical patients and still it looked hopeless
in some cases.

As I walked past a room I caught a part of the ongoing
conversation:

"…operation could lead to massive bleeding…we simply
don't know if he will be able to withstand losing so much blood…" I
assumed that was the doctor speaking.

"Can you do a blood transfusion?"

"I wish we could. We are in short supply of blood and your
son is type O negative.

"That means he can receive any kind of blood right?"

"No ma'am that means he can only receive type O negative
blood."

I felt so sorry for the woman in the room. Even though I
hadn't seen her yet, I know she must have had face of defeat at that

moment. I wanted to see my father, but I knew there was something I had to do. If I didn't, it would haunt me for years.

I knocked on the open door and stepped inside. I excused myself for interrupting and again after I told them I'd accidentally overheard their conversation. I offered to donate some of my blood: I am type O. The woman's face of defeat slightly warmed up and a shine was noticeable in her eye. The doctor looked at me and then at the mother. The doctor said it would be time consuming. Paper work would need to be filed. Permission from the parent must be given. I believe it was just a way for him to say he doesn't need my blood. The mother said she approved of the idea on the spot and would give full permission. Then the doctor explained that my blood would have to be tested to see if it was O negative or positive. If I am positive I wouldn't be able to give the little kid my blood. The doctor didn't say it but I knew they also wanted to test to make sure I didn't have any STD's. No problem there I'd wanted to say. My condition had left me sort of an outcast. Lust and sex had been one of the least important things in my life.

I was led to a small room with a nurse. The nurse asked me a few prescreening questions I could have basically answered no to without even hearing the question. No I don't do drugs. No I don't engage in homosexual activities. No I haven't been outside of the country in the past 3 years. No I have never had Hepatitis. With the questioning done, she pricked my finger and took a sample of my blood. She left the room, leaving me behind with my thoughts.

After a few minutes she returned and gave me the good news: I was type O negative. Of course I knew that though. Donating blood was something I'd picked up when I turned 18. Every possible donation day after that, I'd given blood.

The nurse then cleaned my arm and tied a tourniquet around my bicep. My veins popped up and became clearly visible. She brought the needle out and I almost lost my breath for a second. It was bigger than I imagined. The ones at the Red Cross had been big but that needle had been enormous. My fear of needles hadn't helped much then. I would see it through though. She gets closer to me with the needle and the predominating thought in my head is: Oh my God. This is going to hurt.

J. Carlos Perez

Once the needle was in, it was all down to the time it would take the blood to flow into the plastic bag. The whole process took a little over 20 minutes in which all I had to do was squeeze a black handlebar like tube. Once finished she took out the needle and bandages my arm in purple gauze. I knew the 2 pints of blood I had given would help but it wouldn't be enough if the boy lost a lot of blood. I'd done all I could though so I'd carried on.

On my way out of the room the mother stopped me and thanked me for donating blood so her son could have his operation. She extended her arms and wrapped them around me. At first I was confused but then I hugged her back enjoying the little things.

When I was finally heading back on my way, I found myself with a deep desire to see my father. After seeing my brother it made me realize I will always be my dad's little kid. No matter how old I get my parents will always see me as their child. I might be a man but in their eyes they still see my running around with the same blanket I'd given to my brother. Although my father may not be able to hear me, I still wanted to thank him for everything he'd done to make my childhood the best and for raising me to the best of his ability.

I walked towards the elevator with sweaty hands. My stomach felt weak and my face cold. I began to see yellow dots which turned into nauseating blurs. I'd grabbed for the wall for support but fell to the ground anyways.

I woke up in the same room I had left earlier. The same nurse was waving an alcohol soaked cotton ball in front of my nose. My speech was a little garbled but I think I'd made my point that I was okay and wanted to leave. She'd nodded her head and put her hand on top of mine. It wasn't a sexual advancement. Of that I was sure. She was a young nurse—maybe early twenties. In the world we were living in, small connections with total strangers really made an impact. I'd smiled at her and then left the room. I walked back down to the elevator and rode two stories up.

On the 5th floor, I saw and heard a scene that made my stomach hurt again. I heard screams of pain from patients and I saw doctors doing the best they could to soothe the pain with medication. All their best efforts were not doing much in some cases. It was obvious that the fifth floor had been assigned for the "not

206

going to make it" patients. Struggling to keep going forward, I'd reached my father's room. I knew he wouldn't hear me but out of courtesy I'd knocked on the door. As I walked into the room I heard a sound I had been trying to push out of my head since my first steps in the hospital. I didn't cry; I didn't feel angry. I had accepted the fact that my father might not make it out alive. Listening to the steady tone of the machine had brought calmness to mind. My father was in a better place. Anywhere would have been a better place at the moment. Heaven or hell. I sat down in a chair by the bed and turned off the monitor.

The flash is what I will remember the most. It was otherworldly. It was surreal. It was a reality I had never expected to see in my life time.

J. Carlos Perez

Makayla

The winter-morning breeze was taunting the brave to dare
venture out into its grasp. It's short icy breaths mimicking the cries of
a newborn—one-minute calm and then the next, bellowing out in an
unbearable tempest. Among the hundreds of early risers dressed in
layers—shirt, fleece, sweater, and jacket, Makayla was sitting on a
bench under a barren willow tree, weeping into her hands. Other
students walked by curious about the weeping girl, sparing a second
or two to look at her, but nobody dared stay in the unsheltered open
longer than necessary.

Even though Makayla was dressed for the cold weather, her
face was red around the cheeks and even redder around her nose.
The tears flowing from her eyes inched their way to the tip of her
nose and almost freezing forming miniature icicles.

Fifty feet away, inside the comfort of the warm building, I
stood watching as the world passed her by with no resemblance of
caring. Fresh out of ceramics class, my hands were dry as chalk. I was
halfway through a Twix candy bar and already thinking about
opening the other package of chocolaty perfection in my pocket.
Even though I tried to refrain from eating sweets, I hadn't had
breakfast and needed something to keep me going through the rest of
my classes. For some odd reason, the vending machines never have
something halfway healthy. (I should point that out to someone.)

I reached into my pockets and fished for my strawberry
ChapStick. Car Keys, no; flash drive, no; cell phone, no; ah there it is.
Talking to myself isn't something I do often but I do admit it
happens on the rare occasion. After applying a thin layer of
ChapStick onto my imperfect lips, I ventured out into the cold. I
walked with my hands in the jackets fur lined pockets and my face
turned towards the floor and to the right—away from the wind. As I
got closer to the bench I started to think about what I was doing.
Was I really going to talk to this girl? I'm a shy guy around strangers.
I couldn't just randomly start talking to her. Especially not since she
was crying. Maybe I'd make things worse by popping her bubble.
Could I even do that?

When I got to the bench, feeling like a dumbass with a tinge of confidence, I did what seemed most reasonable. I sat down. Makayla (of course I didn't know her name just yet) glanced my way and stared at me like to say, "*What do you want?*"

Her eyes were red and puffy, swollen from the tears. Black streaks ran from her eyes down her cheeks like a messy watercolor rundown. Even in that condition, she looked superior to the average woman. Her curly brown hair was in front of her, blowing into her face with each strong gust of wind.

Struggling, with no words to say, I reached into my coat pocket and pulled out the unopened candy bar. Makayla was still staring at me, closer to saying "*Are you seriously going to eat a chocolate bar next to me while I cry my eyes out to the world?*" I carefully opened the package, pulled out one of the bars and took a small bite. I then outstretched my arm towards her and asked, "Would you like a piece?"

She thought about it for a minute and then reached for the Twix bar. She took a bit with her perfectly formed mouth and then said, "Thanks, I guess."

Figuring the ice was pretty much broken; I started some conversation with her.

"Is something wrong?" I asked, cautiously thinking ahead of what I might say next.

"Not anything you can help with." She said coldly.

"You never know. I have been known to be very helpful. I mean, I can already tell you're crying because something a guy did to you, right?"

"Maybe, how could you know that?" she inquired.

"Guys are jerks." I plainly stated. A smug look on my face.

"So you're saying you're a jerk?" She raised an eyebrow in a way that almost made my heart skip a beat.

"No."

"Then you're saying you're not a guy." She had a smile on her face now and I knew I was well on my way to cheering her up with the simplest of words.

"I'm a guy all right. I'm just a different type of guy."

"Right I know what you mean. You think with your left nut instead of your right. Or is it vice versa?" Her face had hardened again into the implacable stone fortress it had been when I first sat down.

"Neither. I think with this." I put my finger on my chest and added, "I think with my heart. Plus I am a poet. We poets live in a whole different world than your average man."

She busted out laughing and said, "You picked the wrong day to try to sweet talk your way around me."

"I'm not trying to sweet talk you or anything. I just thought I'd come over here and see if I could help with anything. I thought for someone to be sitting out here in this bitter cold, there must be something seriously bothering them."

"Well something was seriously bothering me."

"I like how you said 'was'. Gives me some hope that maybe I cheered you up a bit."

"Well you weren't doing at bad job at whatever you were doing. I stopped crying if you'd noticed."

"I had. You look gorgeous now. Not that you didn't before."

"Okay now buster. Don't push your luck. You haven't even told me your name yet."

"Oh that's right isn't it? Well my name is Charles. Nice to meet you." I had a cheesy smile on my face but I didn't care. I'd left my comfort zone and went for something I felt was right.

"Nice to meet you too. My name is Makayla. And let's skip this crap I'm not a big fan of formalities. How about we go somewhere and you cheer me up."

"Oh so you're only going to talk to me because you need someone to talk to? Is that what it is?" I said sarcastically.

"No. I'm going to talk to you because I want to see how good of a poet you are. Just because you say you're one doesn't necessarily make you one." There was a glimmer in her eye I hadn't seen before. A faint light once receding into the darkness of her pupils, it now lit up her face.

"Well then, how about we go inside and grab a cup of coffee? I'm sure it would be a good idea to get some hot liquid into your system before you freeze to death out here."

"No."

"I thought you just said…." I started to say blankly.

She leaned in closer to me and whispered, "Ask me again but

this time ask if I want to go get something to eat." And then in an even quieter voice added, "I don't drink coffee."

"Would you like to get something to eat?" I said.

"Why sure. I'd love to." We both laughed at this.

"But before we go ..." I reached towards her face and wiped some of the smeared makeup she had running down her face. "Now we can go."

My Hello Kitty Bracelet

I knew it was going to be a bad day when I woke up and had two thoughts pounding inside me head; begging to come out.

Is the math test today or is it tomorrow?

It's always "today" when you have to ask, isn't it?

Okay then, I guess I better go get my Hello Kitty bracelet.

Most people wouldn't understand why I would look for that bracelet and I don't really care about those people; they don't really know me.

About the bracelet. It's pink, scratched up, and–to get the visual across—from a McDonald's happy meal. I mean, we're talking really cheap. The cost doesn't really matter here, though because I didn't buy it, and that's why it's so valuable to me. It's more of a sentimental values.

The bracelet was given to me by my bestest—an inside joke between us—friend. I don't know why I think the bracelet is lucky, I just do. Every time I am going to do something that will require me to perform exceptionally well to pass—like this math test—I always wear it. It makes me feel loved, more confident. Okay, it's probably dumb, but whatever works, right?

Rolling out of bed, I opened the drawer where I kept it along with every drawing she's made for me, along with a bunch of other stuff. They were all jokes that only made sense to her and me, worthless things except for the immense emotional value they held as memories.

I slid my hand into the usual place where I always left the bracelet, cushioned atop a grey beanie that I wore only once—the first day I straightened my hair.

What? It's not there.

Pushing the mess of papers aside, even tossing some out of the drawer, I still couldn't find it. But—it was always here. How was I supposed to pass my math test without it?

Panicking now, I went out to the living room where my mom was watching some random movie on HBO. "Mom, have you seen my Hello Kitty bracelet?"

"Do you mean the pink one that you keep in the drawer?"

"Yes that one."

"You're obsessed with that thing. You don't need it."

"But—but—you know how much it means to me."

She flicks the channels; trying to avoid the topic from continuing further. "Yeah maybe too much. You think it's the only reason you do well in school, and it's not. You're so smart—why can't you give yourself credit?"

"Fuck, Mom. You've got the best way of making me feel better about myself, by making me feel ten times worse."--sarcasm at its best.

Furious, I slammed my stuff into my backpack and left. I was almost to school—already late—when I realized that I'd forgotten my calculator. That was really going to help me in passing the test; no bracelet, no calculator, not going to pass.

Screw this. I should just skip the whole class. I'm going to fail anyways, without my bracelet. No wait, I'll go, and fail, and show my mom how badly I did. She'll regret what she did then, I bet.

Not my best plan ever, but it wasn't like I had anything else to do.

"You can use your calculator's on the test if you wish"

Oh, I do wish. In fact I would love to use my calculator. Too bad I don't have it. Man, this is the worst. I hate my mom.

When I got home my mom still sitting on the couch watching TV, probably been there all day. Only getting up when her necessities called.

I threw my backpack on the floor; landing with a loud thump, awakening her from her zombie like state. "You happy now? I failed my test."

"You failed? How can you even know that already?"

"Well, I don't know for sure, but you threw away my bracelet, so I'm sure I did." I slumped onto the floor. "Why'd you do that, Mom? It's not just the luck part—you know Laken gave it to me."

"I'm just doing what I see is fit for my son. I'm worried about you."

I rolled my eyes. "Well, I appreciate your way of showing motherly concern. Congratulations, you made your point. Too bad it made me fail my stupid math test. And since you threw it away, it's gone forever."

My mom shifted her weight on the couch; probably to keep your ass from going numb. "I lied."

"What?"

"I lied. I didn't throw your bracelet away; it's right here." She held it up between her thumb and middle finger, twisting it back and forth with the movement of her wrist. Handing it over with a smug expression, she said "Now when you pass that test, it will be because of you and not the bracelet."

I grabbed it away from her. "You're so freaking weird sometimes." I stomped back to my room, still angry but relieved to have the reassuring weight on my bracelet on my wrist.

There is no way that I am going to pass that test. She has no earthly idea what she is talking about.

My math teacher e-mails us the results of our tests that same afternoon. I hate that; I'd be happier waiting until the next day to hear about my miserable failure. Sighing, I clicked open the file. At least after seeing the results I will have a good reason to go scream at my mom.

"Carlos, I am very proud of you," my teacher had written. "I know you've been struggling with math since the beginning, and when I saw you without your calculator, I was very concerned. However, you did very well today, getting an 87. Congratulations! Please remember to bring your calculator tomorrow, though. We are going to start working with something a little more complicated."

My eyes were fixed on the computer screen; my mind looking for a way to make the situation turn in my favor.

Crap

Mom's never going to let me hear the end of this.

Then I remember the bracelet on my wrist. Laken made it for me on our way home one day; I'd almost forgotten about it. It never comes off my hand so I had gotten used to it.

Oh man, mom is really going to like this one. It wasn't the Hello Kitty bracelet after all; it was this one.

I'm glad that's all over.

J. Carlos Perez

Room 408

Walking into room 408 always brought me down. No matter how hard I tried to stay in a positive mood, I always fell into a depressive downing mood. I knew the efforts being put in to save Jordan tough tremendous, things were even looking good for a while, were not going to be enough. Call it a gut feeling. Things always seemed to play out the same in my life. When I finally had something to complete me, it was taken away.

Walking in today was harder than any time before. I knew after today I would never step back into room 408. After today there would be no reason. I always knew this day would come but I never expected it to be this way. I never imagined I would have to be the one.

When I first met Jordan she was standing in the fiction section in Barnes & Nobles reading the summary of Before I Fall by Lauren Oliver. I remember this because I had recently bought and read the book. It was the reason I talked to her in the first place.

She was looking at it and another book—which I have by now forgotten the title, deciding which one she should take. She picked one up and then set it back down to pick up the other one, only to change her mind seconds later. I approached her said "Take them both. Whether you take one or the other you're going to end up wishing you had taken the other."

She looked up at me with a sparkle in her eye, grinned and said "Is that so?" It was that look that won me over. From that day forward I always looked forward to that same smile. It was my way of knowing she was truly satisfied.

That day we'd spent hours sitting in the Starbucks coffee section of Barnes & Nobles, sitting at a table sharing favorite quotes from books over mocha latte. It was nerdy romanticism. I found out that not all beautiful "bring home to mom and dad" girls found Chuck Palahniuk's books bloody and disgusting. She found out not all readers of Cormack McCarthy and Kafka has a loose screw in their head—well maybe mine is a little loose. Life had been perfect for 45 years.

My wife, Jordan, at age 73 had a massive brain hemorrhage, leaving her in a vegetable state, alive only because of the machinery supplying oxygen to her. Not alive by the grace of God rather a piece of junk man invented. The doctors tried all they could but there was nothing they could do. It was a losing battle from the beginning. Perhaps I could have prayed a bit more. One thing is for certain, what I was about to do was final. There was no going back. I had made up my mind. I loved my wife too much to see her suffer anymore.

As I gulped, I could feel the sweat beading down my face. Funny. It isn't even hot inside the hospital. My sweaty hands played with the objects in my pockets interior: keys, ChapStick, a Phillips screw.

I walk to her side and hold her hand to my face. There are tears streaming from my face now as reality sinks into me. It's all too much for me. I always wondered what are last minutes together would be like. I never imagined they would be like this.

I slowly reach for the machine, placing my hand on the radial knob with "off" as one of the settings. Slowly, snail like, I turned it to "off". At the same time I reach into my sport coats inner pocket and pull out the small 9mm pistol. My hand trembles now more than it had before. As the heart monitor starts to lose its uniform beeps, I place the gun to my head. I think back to the day I met her and remember what I said. I rephrase that and say it to God now. "Take us both. Whether you take one or the other you're going to end up wishing you had taken the other."

In the end, nothing matters.

J. Carlos Perez

The Perfect Kiss

You know, I've always gotten what I wanted. Not to say that I'm a megalomaniac or something but when it came to getting things done. I always put my whole behind it to make it happen. There was only one thing that had eluded me all year, well at least until today on the 7th of May.

You see I have this friend, a pretty close friend. But nothing too serious. I guess we were not what each other viewed in our perfect someone. She was beautifully blonde, blue eyed, and gorgeous. Ever since I had seen her at the pools I had fallen in love with her, she was the only lifeguard.

Well as it so happens the only thing that I had not been able to acquire all year was a kiss from those oh so plump lips that she called her own. They had been close to mine many times but they always seemed to vanish right before my eyes.

Many times I wondered how or what I could do to get a taste of those perfect lips, but every time I thought about them my mind went blank. I was too busy thinking about her lips that I forgot to think about how to get them.

Summer was fast approaching and I knew that I would have very little chances left if I did not think fast. So this morning as I was eating my breakfast cereal it hit me. Well actually it got stuck in me. The cereal I had been eating had gotten stuck in my throat. Thank God I knew how to do the Heinrich maneuver on myself. Right then as I was coughing from lack of air I realized what I could do to get those perfect lips that had eluded me for so long.

When I got to school this morning, I saw her at the same spot she always was. It was the same spot that I went to every morning. I swallowed all my nervousness and went up to her as usual. We were talking like usual except this time I was eating one of those cereal bar things that for some reason so many people think are healthy. We talked for a while until I faked it. There was nothing stuck in my throat but I sure ass hell pretended there was. My face turned blue, I started coughing, I fell to the ground to make it look even batter.

Even though I had my eyes closed I could feel someone move forward towards me. (I should have kept my eyes open) It was happening just as I had envisioned it would. And then I felt them, those oh so perfect lips. They touched mine and mine touched them. It was all-perfect, a perfect moment of bliss in a world plagued by destruction and hate. Even though they were just preforming CPR on me it felt just as well. Soon enough I got tired of that and went for it. Kissing those lips like I had never kissed any other lips before. Everything was going well, at least until I opened my eyes. Oh what a surprise was in store for me when I opened my eyes. The person who's perfect lips had eluded me for so long where not the lips that had come into contact with mine just merely seconds ago. Instead they were those of the assistant principle who happened to be walking by when I faked it. I mean I'm not complaining the kiss was great, but the principle herself. Well just to be nice and make her look a little more....well, attractive, I will compare her to the dead decomposed fetus of a goat.

Geez, all my hard work and for what? A kiss from an old lady. I was so embarrassed, and of course it didn't end just like that. Apparently, I had broken many school rules with my little act. It landed me in detention for the rest of the day and the week that followed.

Well this afternoon as school was letting out. Who else but the lifeguard herself was standing by my car. I was anticipating ridicule and jestering, but none of that occurred. I did not even say a word before she advanced on me and gave me the kiss I had been craving since so long.

J. Carlos Perez

The Proposal

There are a couple of things a woman never forgets. Among other things, forgetting to pick up your kid after soccer practice, after she deliberately told you she would be at a meeting, will have you sleeping on your side of the bed motionless. That of course is later on in the relationship and lower down on the hierarchy of unforgettable moments for your special someone.

Justin Wheeler's relationship with Juliet Simms was not that far advanced but everything pointed towards it. Not the forgetting the kid at soccer practice part, the part about being married. Justin and Juliet were 20 and 19, and they both agreed they would wait until marriage to have sexual relations. A choice not many young people do during these days but they thought it held a touch of romanticism—waiting for one special person, through lust and desire, until that one night after the wedding.

For Justin, everything was about making every possible moment he spent with Juliet something they could talk about once they were old and withered, rocking outside on the porch in handmade chairs. The moment he saw as being the most important, well yet to be moment, was the wedding proposal. Popping the question is romantic in itself but the way he did it had to be new. He didn't want to do an overly clichéd theatric like having a waiter put the ring in her cup of champagne at a fancy restaurant.

He had another idea in mind; in fact, he was 25 jumps into the idea. That's what it took to get a USPA A License, 25 jumps—that is, if all the requirements were met during those 25 jumps. After he got the A license he would be able to jump without supervision, pack his own parachute, and engage in basic group jumps. That's what he wanted. He didn't want to jump off a plane and have Juliet jump tandem (tied to the front) with an instructor. He knew she wouldn't jump solo and first-time jumpers couldn't jump solo anyways. So the best workaround was for him to get the license so she could jump tandem with him. He wanted to pop the question 14,000 feet into the air with the wind pushing against their bodies.

After picking out a ring and reserving a plane, he mentioned the idea of skydiving to Juliet. She'd gone over to his house and they were watching Man Vs. Wild—funny, he was jumping out of a plane himself.

"Are you crazy? I'm not getting anywhere near a plane with a parachute. You might be crazy enough to do it but not me. Nuh uh buster, not me."

"Come on, it'll be fun."

"Planes were made as transportation devices. It's not safe to jump out of a moving vehicle you know."

And then as a final attempt to get her to go, he used the negotiation card. "Do you remember that concert you wanted to go? Broken something?"

"Brokencyde!"

"Yes that one." He didn't like the band at all, considered them a waste of space. "Well if you do this one thing with me, I'll go to that and any other concert you want me to go to. Or we can go to one of those art shows you're always talking about."

"Hmm let me think about this. Brokencyde or art show." That was good, Justin thought. She was thinking about which boring activity to do. That meant she would go. He prayed she would choose the art show. Anything at all would be better than Brokencyde. "It's a tough decision, maybe we could do both?" Juliet lifted her face up a bit and made her irresistible puppy face look.

Well hell, at least she'll jump, he thought. "Okay, you got it. We'll go to the concert and the art show, but first we jump. I have reservations for this weekend."

"Sly devil you. You had this all planned out didn't you?" She laughed and then decided it would be best if she went home. She knew if she stayed much longer she would end up naked on the right side of his bed. No good.

That weekend, Justin picked up Juliet at her apartment and drove towards the skydiving center. The small airport wasn't too far away from where they lived, at most 30 minutes. On the way there though, Justin had to swerve to avoid a crow which flew out in front of the Suzuki Forenza. Weird behavior? Bad Omen?

At the hanger, Justin introduced Juliet to Tyrone the pilot. "Juliet, this is Tyrone. He's been my pilot since the first time I came here. Tyrone, this is my girlfriend Juliet."

"Nice to meet you." Juliet said extending her arm.

"The pleasure is mine. I've heard so many great things about you."

"You have?" Juliet gave Justin a quick smirk.

"I think we should get a move on." Justin quickly interjected. He was afraid Tyrone would accidentally let something slip about Justin's plan on proposing up in the air. After 25 jumps Justin and Tyrone had got to known each other pretty well, sharing drinks every other week.

"Are you sure this is safe? Maybe you should let Tyrone or somebody else to check the equipment before we jump."

"No worried there mam." Tyrone responded for him. "Justin is one of the fastest learners I've seen around here in a while. He knows what he is doing."

"You see, now come on lets go."

A little after 90 seconds, Tyrone was piloting the plane down the runway and into the sky. While he steadily ascended the plane to the jumping height, Justin tried to get Juliet excited. Once the plane reached 14,000 feet and leveled off, Justin opened the door and said some final words to Juliet. "It's pretty cold out there, probably below 40 so hold on tight babe." And then, they were off.

The first initial moments were filled with Juliet screams. At first from sheer fright but then later from excitement. If they had been free falling they could have reached over 100 MPH hours but instead they were going a moderate 63.

At around 11,000 feet, Justin decided it was time to propose. For safety he wanted to open the parachute at around 5,000 feet and wanted to give her some time to take the moment in as well. He reached into a pocket and produced the ring. Justin then reached in front of Juliet face, holding the ring in front of her face. He couldn't see her reaction but once they'd gotten done he'd look at the recording from her helmet cam. "Will you marry me?!" he screamed to be heard over the sound of wind hurling past them.

"YESSSS!" He could hear her response flying directly to his ears.

With the moment over, Justin could only speed up their decent up so he could kiss her once on the ground.

Just to be safe, Justin pulled the parachute string a little before five thousand feet. Nothing. The parachute didn't come out. He pulled again but still nothing happened. "Babe, you know I love you right?" He screamed down at her.

"Yea, I love you too, but you better open the parachute. Aren't we getting a little low?"

"I'm sorry babe."

And before they hit the ground, Justin thought to himself, "At least I don't have to go to the Brokencyde concert."

The Sugar Cookie Icing

He was a young man, 17 years of age. He was standing by an old dogwood tree that never seemed to lose its beauty with a sugar cookie in his pocket talking… seducing… enamoring… a 15 year old. Time was slowed down by the beating of their hearts. Each second lasting longer than the last as their hearts slowed down. He pointed behind the girl telling her he had seen a deer running through the woods behind them. He told her of its beauty comparing its graceful walking to everything he loved about her. She smiled, knowing it could not be true. She'd never seen a deer in those parts of town in all her life. Why would there be a deer randomly walking by then? Yet curiosity got the best of her and she turned. As she turned her head in an effort to see the supposed deer, the young man smeared some of the icing from the sugar cookies on his finger, wiping it on her face as she turned back around, directly on her lips.

She had been surprised by the sudden movement of his hand near her face. Even though they were not dating, she felt so in tune with him. He's hand feeling rough yet tender against her soft pale skin. She'd thought he would do that if she turned around to look for the deer but the thought hadn't stopped her...part of her wanted him to do it.

He smiled at her as she took her left index finger and tried to wipe the icing from her face. Though she was trying, something in him sensed she didn't exactly want to take it off herself. She had gotten most of it off and was going to get the rest when he offered to take the remaining icing off. With soft thread he placed his hand upon her face, wiping her luscious hazel hair back behind her ear. Looking deeply into her eyes he inched his way closer and kissed her ...gently...romantically...perfectly...so full of love. Why they hadn't admitted it to each other before can't be certain. Perhaps both wanted their friendship to remain unhindered by the what ifs of the future. But what it couldn't be denied much longer...they were both secretly in love with each other. The moment seemed perfect. A Kodak moment only found within a Nicholas Sparks book, until...he opened his eyes and realized he still had the icing on his finger. The icing still waiting for him to get her to turn away so he could wipe the green icing on her lips.

J. Carlos Perez

Vote

I get up early in the morning, driven solely by the thoughts of the day ahead. I turn on the TV, not watching but listening to every growing lie told by the media. Exasperated by this, I turn the TV off and turn on the radio. I don't listen to FM or AM stations because the music played on the stations are censored. Instead I listen to the music the artist intends for me to hear. I get dressed; I put on my best attire, and head out to work. At work I look around and think to myself that I probably got the job because of my ethnicity. Was I the best man for the job? I don't know. I like to think so everyday when I step in the door but as far as I know I am just there to please policy. During my lunch break I buy a newspaper and coffee and read the headline stories. I see politicians throwing dirt at each other trying to get me to vote for them but does it matter whom I vote for. No matter who I vote for today it's not me who gets to choose who the next president is. The Electoral College is the one that formally picks the president; my vote is simply going to be used as a statistic. I go back to work, finish up and then I go to the voting center. Looking at the ballot there are only two parties; only two. I would like to have more of a choice but it doesn't matter. I don't really care who wins. I am just exercising my right to vote. I cast my ballot and head home. After a day like this I simply turn on the TV and sit down on my couch. Even though I turned on the TV, I don't watch it. Instead I grab the latest James Patterson book from my shelf and read. The TV is on only for what it is useful; background noise

❖

www.ingramcontent.com/pod-product-compliance
Lightning Source LLC
Chambersburg PA
CBHW050521260626
47157CB00004B/1418